PRINCIPLES OF
COMPUTER SCIENCE
JAVA EDITION
• KEN HOWARD •

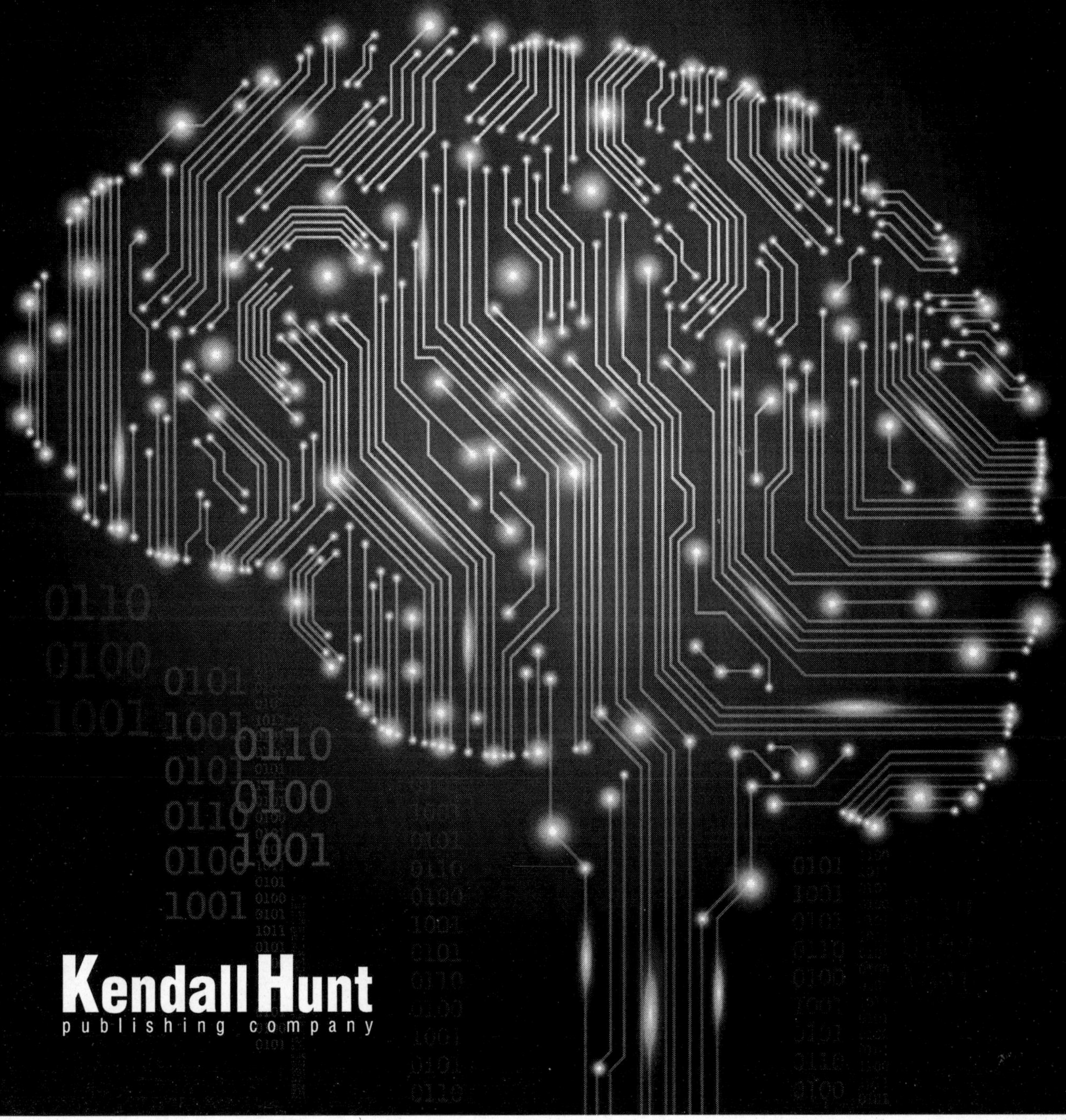

Kendall Hunt
publishing company

Kendall Hunt
publishing company

www.kendallhunt.com

Send all inquiries to:
4050 Westmark Drive
Dubuque, IA 52004-1840

ISBN 978-1-4652-2252-7

Printed in the United States of America
10 9 8 7 6 5 4 3 2 1

CONTENTS

CHAPTER 1

INTRODUCTION

Computer software is becoming an increasingly important part of most people's lives. Just reflect back on the last two hours of your life. How much computer software did you interface with? Did you answer your phone, send a text message, check email, or edit a document with a word processor? Those are the obvious ones. How about did you drive in a car, adjust the thermostat, turn on the microwave, or open the refrigerator?

Software is either directly or indirectly a part of almost everything in our lives. Even the most non-technical thing you can think of—perhaps a good old fashioned #2 pencil is associated with a lot of software: the machines that created it, the inventory software that tracks the raw materials used to manufacture it, the supply chain software that got it shipped to where it was sold, and so on.

The non-profit foundation Code.org predicts that by the year 2020, there will be 1.4 million Computer Science related job openings, and only 400,000 Computer Science students. That's a one million job deficit. Even if you exclude specialized jobs and those requiring extensive job experience, there is still a huge gap between job openings and people qualified to fill them. In an economy with so much uncertainty, the field of Computer Science appears to be a very stable place to be employed.

BRIEF HISTORY OF COMPUTERS

The history of computers isn't easily described as as a singular linear series of dependent events. Early computers often derived ideas from a small number of predecessors, but innovation nowadays occurs across a vast number of different concurrent paths. The purpose of this section is simply to highlight a few key milestones in the evolution of computing.

THE ABACUS

The abacus is often referred to as the world's first computer. The abacus dates back as far as 2700 BC in Mesopotamia. These devices have taken varied forms over the years, but the function is basically the same: the colored beads represent numbers, and their placement on the rack helps facilitate math calculations. Variations in different cultures include variations on size, numbering systems (e.g., decimal, hexadecimal, base 20), and orientation of the beads.

The Abacus

NAPIER'S BONES

John Napier was a Scottish mathematician and scientist who discovered logarithms. In the early 1600s he developed a variation of the abacus that became known as Napier's bones.

The "bones" were actually 10 rods that contained the multiplication tables for each digit from 0 to 9. Each rod by itself provided simple multiplication table results, but the real power was when rearranging the bones to represent a large number, and using the bone values to determine the multiplication results. Napier's bones could also help solve division problems.

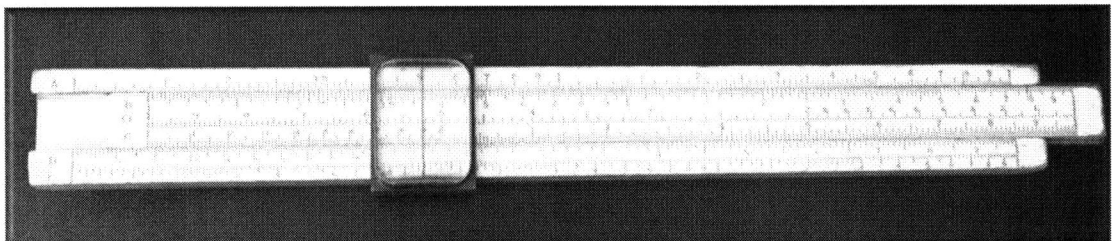

THE SLIDE RULE

Shortly after Napier discovered logarithms, around 1620, a calculating device called a slide rule was developed by Edmund Gunter that was able to aid in the calculation of logarithms, multiplication, division, roots and powers, and trigonometry functions. The slide rule remained an important and popular tool for almost 350 years, until it was replaced by readily available computers and the electronic calculator.

The Slide Rule

PASCAL'S CALCULATOR

In 1642, Blaise Pascal invented the first mechanical calculator. While the user of Napier's Bones had to carry digits manually when performing multiplication, Pascal's calculator was able to carry digits automatically.

JACQUARD WEAVING LOOM

In 1801, Joseph Marie Jacquard invented a computing device with a purpose other than simplifying math calculations. A power of computers is their ability to manage repetition of instructions with consistently, predictable results. Creating textiles with weaving looms involves many repetitious steps. Jacquard creating a sequence of wooden tiles with holes drilled in them that were "read" by the machine. The arrangement of holes on each wooden tile directed the loom to perform a specific function. Connecting several of these tiles with a sequence of encoded instructions cause the machine to quickly and accurately replicate multiple copies of the same textile pattern.

BABBAGE DIFFERENCE ENGINE

In the mid-1800s, Charles Babbage took the mechanical calculator to the next level. His Difference Engine was much larger and more powerful, and was powered by steam. Babbage was the first inventor to introduce the concept of separating memory for the program instructions from memory for the data being processed. His machine also supported conditional logic and had

Jacquard Weaving Loom

a separate component for inputting and outputting data. These concepts became core elements of the architecture of modern computers.

THE HOLLERITH CARD

In late 1890, Herman Hollerith worked for the U.S. Census Office and employed the use of a device he had built and patented while in college. His machine was able to tabulate data that was encoded by punching holes in cards. The machine could read the values encoded on the cards in a very similar manner to how Jacquard's weaving loom worked. The 1880 census had taken 8 years to complete, and with Hollerith's invention, the 1890 census was completed in just one year.

Babbage Difference Engine

The Hollerith Card continued to be used as a form of secondary memory for almost a century after its introduction. As recently as the 1980s, programmers would encode their program instructions on a set of cards that could be read into a computer's primary memory and executed.

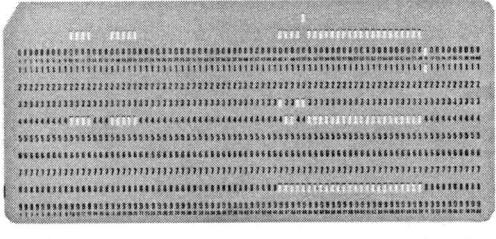

Herman Hollerith's company merged with three other companies in 1911 to form the company that would later be renamed International Business Machines, or IBM.

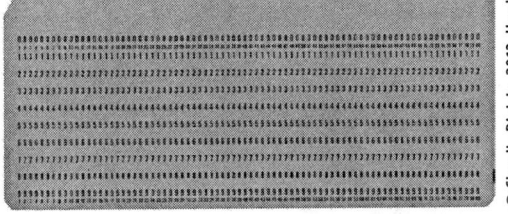
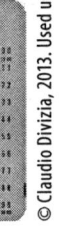

ENIAC

A computer named the ENIAC (Electronic Numerical Integrator and Computer) was built in the 1940s, and was the world's first general purpose computer. This means it was not hard-wired to serve a single purpose, but it was programmable and could be used for solving a multitude of problems. Funding for development of the ENIAC came from the U.S. Army, and it eventually became the "brains" behind the development of the hydrogen bomb.

UNIVAC

The UNIVAC was the first computer developed for use as a business tool. It was designed by the inventors of the ENIAC. The first customer to purchase a UNIVAC was the U.S. Census Bureau in 1951. The first buyer that wasn't associated with a U.S. government agency was Metropolitan Life in 1954.

The ENIAC

One of the developers of the UNIVAC was Grace Hopper, who became a pioneer in computer programming. Hopper developed the first compiler for the UNIVAC, and she later collaborated to develop a computer language called COBOL, which is still used (although with decreasing frequency) today. The picture to the right shows Grace Hopper using one of the devices she worked on. She is often credited with discovering the first computer bug (a moth stuck to a Hollerith Card) but this attribution has been disputed. Nevertheless, it's a fun story. In 1969, the Data Processing Management Association awarded Hopper its first "Computer Science Man of the Year Award" (ironically.)

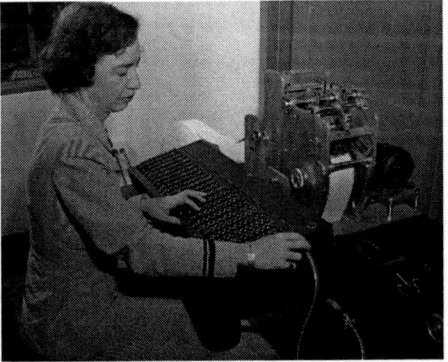

MICROPROCESSOR CHIP

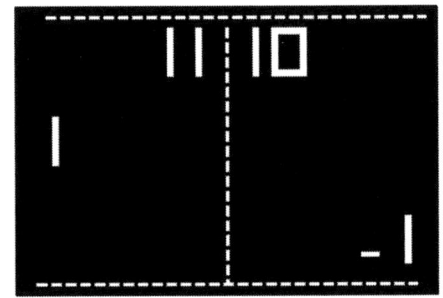

In 1971, Intel Corporation introduced the first commercially available microprocessor. This invention allowed computers to be developed that were faster, easier to maintain, and more reliable. One of the first commercial applications that used the Intel chip was the game of Pong, developed by Atari Corporation.

This was the start of accelerated revolutionary advancements in accessible computing—Devices that were affordable by businesses, and later by home consumers.

One of the co-founders of Intel, Gordon Moore, wrote a paper where he described the density of an integrated circuit measured in its number of components. Moore stated that the density had doubled every year from 1958 (when the integrated circuit was invented) until 1965, the year Moore wrote the paper. Moore's invention of the microprocessor fueled the continuation of this trend. The 18-month doubling cycle was coined as "Moore's Law," and continues to this day. The increased density of processors has led to the evolution of faster and more powerful computers for about the same (or less) cost.

PERSONAL COMPUTERS

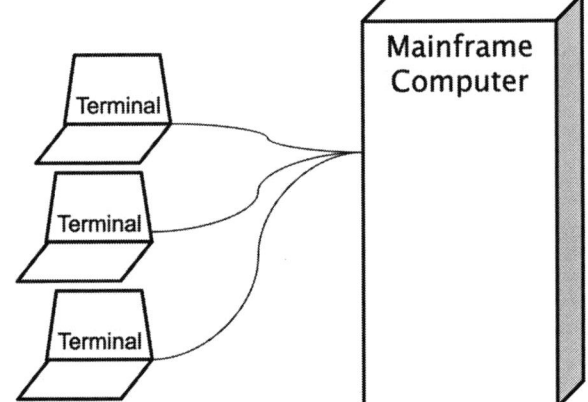

From the 1950s through the early 1980s business computing comprised of a large centrally located computers with multiple monitors and keyboards connected to it. These devices were referred to as "dumb" terminals because they didn't have a processor or memory. They all shared use of one large powerful computer.

These mainframe computers were an evolution of the architecture of the ENIAC and the UNIVAC. This provided a way for many people to sit at their desk and share the use of a computer.

Intel's introduction of the microprocessor chip facilitated the development of smaller "personal" computers. The first of these, developed in the 1970s, didn't offer much in the way of software. As a result, they were used primarily by hobbyists. The Radio Shack TRS-80 and the Apple II were introduced in 1977 and both became popular with early adopters.

From that point on, several other personal computers were marketed. Later in the chapter you'll read about Visicalc, the first spreadsheet software. This introduction of the spreadsheet and word processing software created an explosion of sales of personal computers to businesses.

Radio Shack TRS-80 (circa 1977)

MOBILE COMPUTING

The next set of revolutions in computer hardware revolved around unchaining the computer from the desk. The first portable computers were introduced in the 1980s, and as processors continued to shrink and portable power (battery) technology improved, smaller portable computers were able to become mainstream. Today, the sale of mobile computing devices has far outpaced the sale of desktop devices.

Another catalyst of mobile computing has been remote access to the network. While the mainframe computer architecture had "dumb" terminals hard wired to a central computer, current architecture includes smart devices (with a CPU and memory) connected wirelessly to other smart devices.

The development of the Internet, which evolved based on a number of innovations over a 30 year period from the 1960s to the 1990s, provided the ability for computers anywhere in the world to connect to and communicate with any other computer on the vast network.

EVOLUTION OF LANGUAGES

A thorough description of the history of computer languages would fill volumes. Essentially, any form of instruction given to a computer to do something is specified in some language the computer can understand. In Jacquard's weaving loom, the language was holes in specific locations on a wooden tile. Hollerith used a similar model to communicate with his census tabulator, using hole punched cards.

Programs that instruct a computer to follow a multi-step process required a language that a human could understand, but that could be mapped to a language the computer could understand. The first generation of these languages were not intuitive: Program instructions sent specific signals to the computer hardware directly. This was referred to as *machine language*.

To move the programmer a step away from the hardware, a more generic language called *assembly language* was used. Programmers could write instructions in assembly language without having to know the underlying details of the hardware it was communicating with.

Using this same strategy, a generation of programming languages was developed that allowed a programmer to write instructions in a format that was easily readable and understood by humans. The first of these included FORTRAN, LISP, and COBOL.

From that point on, all languages were variations on the same underlying theme: Finding ways that are intuitive to the programmer, and that communicate efficiently with the underlying hardware. New languages emerge regularly which offer enhanced ease of use and/or capabilities from their predecessors. In this book we'll learn programming using language that's been around for a while and is still a popular choice with software developers: Java.

COMPUTER HARDWARE DETAILS

We're often exposed to advertising for enticing new hardware- the iPhone, the Galaxy, the Mac, iPad, Dell's latest laptop, etc. Realistically, though, the hardware would be boring and useless without software.

Back in 1979, a couple MIT students named Dan Bricklin and Bob Frankston developed the first spreadsheet program named *Visicalc* which they developed to work on the Apple II computer. That single program sold over 700,000 copies. More importantly, the Visicalc spreadsheet single handedly catapulted the personal computer from a niche hobbyist toy into a bonafide business tool. Essentially, Visicalc sold computers. Without it, it was an expensive piece of hardware with little (to no) value.

Hardware is important—without it, the software would have nothing to run on. However, it's often the software that sells the device. When Apple dazzles us with announcements of it's new products, they spend very little time boasting about the hardware features. Instead, they spend most of their time showing off what its software can do.

The desktop computer has become such as prominent business tool that it's difficult to imagine working in any type of white collar job without using a computer most, if not all, the time.

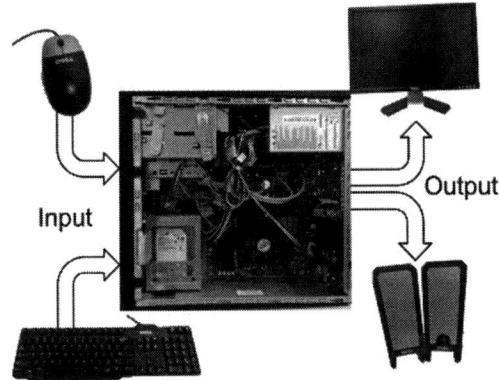

Laptop computers are becoming increasingly popular as their prices have come down, and workers desire the portability.

The component parts of desktop and laptop computer are the same for the most part, although it's easier to open a desktop computer and peek inside.

The part of the computer that does the processing work actually has a very small footprint. A lot of the hardware is there to service you, the user, to get data into the system or get data out of the system. The picture below depicts two of the most common input and output devices on desktop computers: The keyboard and mouse (input) and the display and speakers (output.)

THE CENTRAL PROCESSING UNIT

Inside the computer we find a very small but powerful component called the central processing unit, or CPU. This is where all the math and logic processing is centered. Since this can become a bottleneck, modern computers are fitted with multiple CPUs that process instructions concurrently. When you hear of a computer with a quad-core processor, that means it has four CPU chips.

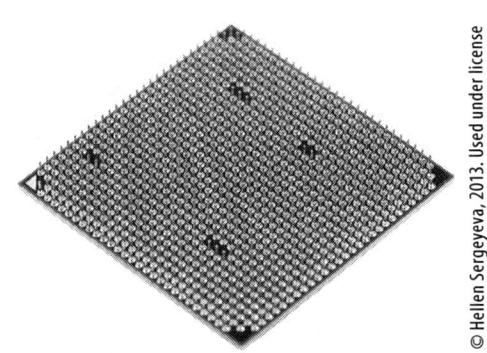

© Hellen Sergeyeva, 2013. Used under license from Shutterstock, Inc.

Each CPU is comprised of three main parts: The control unit, the ALU or Arithmetic and Logic Unit, and Registers (see *Memory* below.)

MEMORY

When executing programs, there is a need to remember, or store, information. There are three types of memory in a computer's hardware:

1. *Registers*: There are very small memory spaces contained on the CPU. They are used to remember a small number of pieces of information (usually numbers) that are used during calculations or other processing.

2. *Primary Memory:* This is also referred to as Random Access Memory, or RAM. This is volatile memory that remembers as long as the computer's power is turned on, and it gets erased each time a computer is shut down. We use RAM to contain the instructions of a computer program we are running, as well as information that program may capture, calculate, or process in some other way.

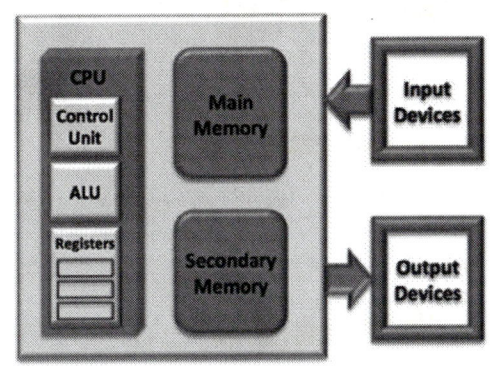

3. *Secondary Memory:* This is memory that is non-volatile. It continues to be retain its information when the computer is turned off. Secondary memory usually takes the form of a hard drive, solid state drive, USB stick, or a burned CD/DVD.

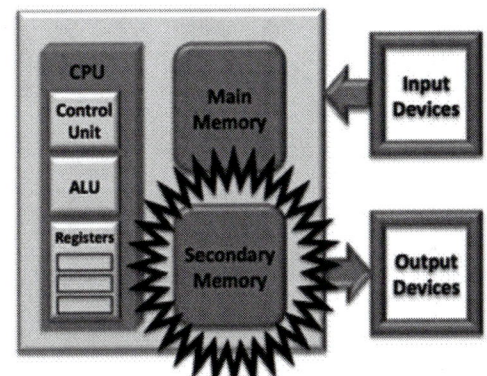

Combining the CPU, Primary Memory and Secondary Memory, along with input and output devices, our computer is equipped to host and run software.

LARGE SCALE COMPUTERS

You may never see many of the computers you use on a regular basis. Whenever you check your email, connect to a website, check the weather, etc., you likely using large scale computers. You may actually be using your desktop, laptop, or mobile device, but the actual work to produce what you see is often handled on very large computers locked in a temperature controlled room somewhere.

Large-scale computers take many forms and come from a variety of vendors. Some are single large

computers called mainframes, while others are clusters of smaller computers that are bundled to behave as a large computer. The hardware components are the same as are found on smaller computers, only scaled up with more capacity to handle many concurrent users.

PURPOSE OF COMPUTER SOFTWARE

At its core, computer software has four basic capabilities:

1. Accept input of information/data

   This could include a human entering data on a keyboard, touch screen, or some other type of device with buttons, keys, dials, etc. This data could be retained temporarily for a single purpose, or it could be retained longer-term for later retrieval and use.

2. Send information/data

Information may be sent to a device such as a monitor, TV, projector or printer. It could also be sent to another computer program on the same computer or on a different computer.

3. Manipulate data

Computer software is great for performing simple to highly complex math functions. It can also transform non-numeric data such as alphabetizing lists, adding prefixes or suffixes, deleting letters or words, etc.

4. Manage flow control

Computer software can be set up to repeatedly do multiple steps in a predetermined order. Additionally, certain steps may repeat while others only happen in certain conditions.

Everything we'll learn to do as we learn computer programming will fall into one of these four categories. Think about computer software you have used, and try to think of things it does for each of the four categories. Not all software does all four of these things, but all software does at least one of them.

A computer program is a set of ordered instructions for a computer to carry out. If you think of a robot, which is a form of a computer, the instructions are tangible and visible. If you instruct the robot to take five steps forward, turn 90 degrees to the right, take 10 more steps, etc., you can witness every step in the process.

When listing a series of instructions for a complex calculation, however, it can be difficult to step through each discrete step of the instructions. A set of instructions to solve the same type of problem with different sets of data is called an algorithm. Much of the work we do when writing computer software involves developing algorithms.

DEVELOPING ALGORITHMS TO SOLVE PROBLEMS

In High School Algebra class, students are taught how to develop equations to solve problems. For example, if we are presented with $X = Y + 5$, and we are asked to determine the value of X if the value of Y is 2, we can easily perform the calculation and determine that the value of X is 7.

This type of problem is the simplest form of algorithm. Through simple substitution of a single value, we are able to determine the solution. Here's a slightly more complex (albeit still very simple) problem that requires some deductive reasoning:

- Spot hid bones in the back yard
- Johnny watched Spot and wants to determine how many bones Spot hid
- There are fewer than 6
- There are more than 3
- There are not 4
- How many bones did Spot hide?

Through deduction, and application of all the information provided, the solution (5 bones) can be deduced. A spreadsheet is a great tool for developing and testing algorithms to solve problems. For practice, try developing algorithms using a spreadsheet (Microsoft Excel, Google Sheets, OpenOffice Calc, etc.) for the following problems:

Problem 1: Area of a Circle

Calculate the area of a circle, given any value of diameter.

Notes:

Area= $\pi * \text{radius}^2$
Estimate π using 22/7
Diameter = Radius * 2

Problem 2: Discount

During a special sales at a store, a 10% discount is taken on purchase over $10.00. Write a program that asks for the amount of purchases, then calculates the discounted price (if applicable.)

Notes:

A boolean test is an expression that evaluates to *true* or *false*
You'll need this to implement conditional logic:
- <u>Excel</u>: *if(boolean-test, [value-if-true], [value-if-false])*
- <u>Google</u>: *if(boolean-test, then-true-value, otherwise-false-value)*
- <u>OpenOffice</u>: *if(boolean-test; true-value; false-value)*

Problem 3: Planetary Age

It takes the Earth one year to orbit the Sun, while Mercury makes the journey in 0.24 Earth years, and the former planet Pluto orbits the sun in 248.6 Earth years.

Create a spreadsheet that lists all eight planets in our Solar System (plus Pluto). Create formulas to determine how old you would be on each of the planets relative to your Earth years.

You may need to use the Internet to research the planet names and each planet's orbiting duration.

Problem 4: Apples

How many apples does Tommy have? Jane has four times as many apples as Tommy, but never more than 10.

Joe has at least one apple, other wise Joe has the amount that four times Tommy's number of apples exceeds 10.

How many apples do Jane and Joe have if Tommy has 1? 5? 8? 50?

Problem 5: Annual Raise

James earns a salary of $50,000/year. He expects to get a 5% raise at the end of this year, 4.9% raise at the end of the second year, etc... with a 0.1% reduction in his raise each year.

Using formulas, calculate James' salary at the end of each year for ten years.

Match the output shown to the right →

	Raise	Salary
NOW		$ 50,000.00
Year 1	5.00%	$ 52,500.00
Year 2	4.90%	$ 55,072.50
Year 3	4.80%	$ 57,715.98
Year 4	4.70%	$ 60,428.63
Year 5	4.60%	$ 63,208.35
Year 6	4.50%	$ 66,052.72
Year 7	4.40%	$ 68,959.04
Year 8	4.30%	$ 71,924.28
Year 9	4.20%	$ 74,945.10
Year 10	4.10%	$ 78,017.85

Problem 6: The Bridge

This is a classic bridge crossing problem that has been around for many years. It has gone by different names, with different constraints, but the basic problem is the same:

A group of four people has to cross a bridge. It is dark, and they have to light the path with a flashlight. No more than two people can cross the bridge simultaneously, and the group has only one flashlight. It takes different time for the people in the group to cross the bridge:

- Annie crosses the bridge in 1 minute
- Bob crosses the bridge in 2 minutes
- Carl crosses the bridge in 5 minutes
- Dorothy crosses the bridge in 10 minutes

How can the group cross the bridge in 17 minutes?

Try solving this problem without assistance. You could try brute force—try every conceivable combination until you find the one that gets everyone to the other side in 17 minutes. However, if you think algorithmically, you could develop a pattern for solving multiple problems like this, even if the values are changed.

What if you weren't given the target time of 17 minutes? What if the duration of each player was changed? If the problem was stated: Find the minimum amount of time it takes four people and one torch to cross the bridge, could you develop a step-by-step process to solve it for any four values? If so, you are well on your way to thinking like a computer programmer!

CHAPTER 2

BASIC JAVA PROGRAMMING

An Internet search of the timeline of computer programming languages will yield hundreds of languages. We could fill up an entire textbook describing the evolution of programming languages and comparing/contrasting them. Suffice it to say, Java is one of a handful of languages that are currently very popular. Before we start learning to program in Java, we'll explore its architecture a bit, which will help you understand why it's such a popular choice.

COMPILING PROGRAMS

A computer program is a set of ordered instructions that tell the computer what to do. These instructions are written in a language that a human can understand, but they are not directly understandable by the computer. In most programming languages, the human-readable code must be converted to a format the computer understands. This step is called *compiling* a program.

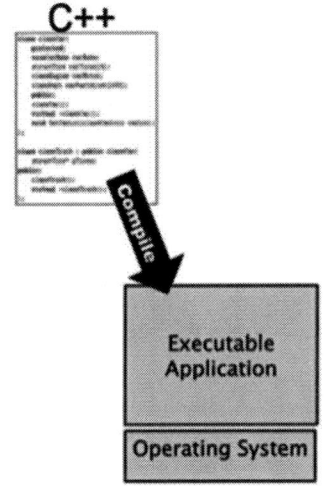

In a popular language such as C++, the result of compiling the source code is a non-human readable format that *can* be understood by the underlying operating system. However, the compiler must convert the code into a format that one specific operating system can understand. For example, if a program is compiled to work on a computer running the Windows operating system, that same program will *not* work on a Mac or on a Linux machine. The source code must be compiled separately with compilers that can generate software that is compatible with those operating systems.

This can be a bit of a burden for software developers who want their program to run on multiple platforms. That is the impetus for the architecture of the Java programming language and runtime environments.

JAVA ARCHITECTURE

With Java, a layer has been added that sits between the operating system and the executable application. This additional layer speaks the language of compiled Java code, and it also speaks the language of the host operating system. This layer is called the *Java Virtual Machine*, or *JVM*.

Once a Java program has been compiled, the compiled Java program can be run on any host operating system that has a compatible *JVM*.

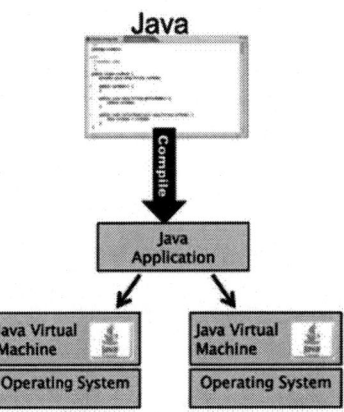

This allows a program to be written and compiled once, and distributed to a variety of platforms. A Java programmer doesn't have to create a unique version of a program for every platform it will be used on.

This "write once, run everywhere" architecture is very powerful. When Java was first developed in 1995, the "run everywhere" benefit wasn't realized because JVM's didn't exist for many platforms. However, as Java became more popular, most operating systems started to ship with a compatible JVM.

The true power of Java is the number of platforms it supports. The vast majority of computers are not desktop or laptop computers. Most computing power can be found in DVD players, home appliances, cars, machines, etc. Many, many hardware platforms include a compatible *JVM* so the logic of those devices can be developed in Java. This is why there is such a huge demand for Java programming skills in the job market.

YOUR FIRST PROGRAM

To get started programming in Java, you'll need a Java compiler and a *Java Virtual Machine* (*JVM*) on your computer. See instructions in the appendix to download and install them.

For now, we'll do all programming using simple text editors that come with your computer, and we'll compile and run those programs using either a Terminal window (Mac) or a CMD window (Windows.) Note that these instructions may vary a bit for your computer based on the operating system version you are running.

STEP 1: Create the Source Code

Windows users: Go to Spotlight and open the program called Notepad.

Mac users: Go to Start and open the program called Textedit.

Enter the following in a new text file:

```
//A Very Simple Example
    class ExampleProgram
    {
            public static void main(String[] args)
            {
            System.out.println("I'm a Simple Program");
            }
    }
```

STEP 2: Save the File

Make sure your text editor is set to "plain" vs. "rich" text format before saving the file. Find a location to store the source code on your computer. You may want to create a folder somewhere that's easy to navigate to. Save your file in that folder with the name *ExampleProgram.java*.

Note: Java is case sensitive, so make sure your capitalization on the filename matches the above exactly as show.

STEP 3: Compile the Program

For this step, you'll need to open a terminal window (Mac) or a CMD window (Windows):

Windows users: Go to Spotlight and enter Terminal.

Mac users: Go to Start and enter CMD.

At this point, you'll need to learn some basic command line navigation. See the appendix for a list of commonly used commands.

Using a combination of ls (Mac) or dir (Windows) to view the contents of a folder, and cd (both platforms) to change directory, navigate to the folder that contains the *ExampleProgram.java* file you just created. When you have found it, type in the following at the terminal/cmd prompt to compile your program:

```
javac ExampleProgram.java
```

Remember that this is case sensitive, so watch your capitalization. If that runs correctly, you should see a new file named *ExampleProgram.class* appear in your directory. This *class* file is the compiled version of your program that can be interpreted and executed by the *JVM*.

The following example (Windows operating system) shows a directory listing, compiling our program, then running our program:

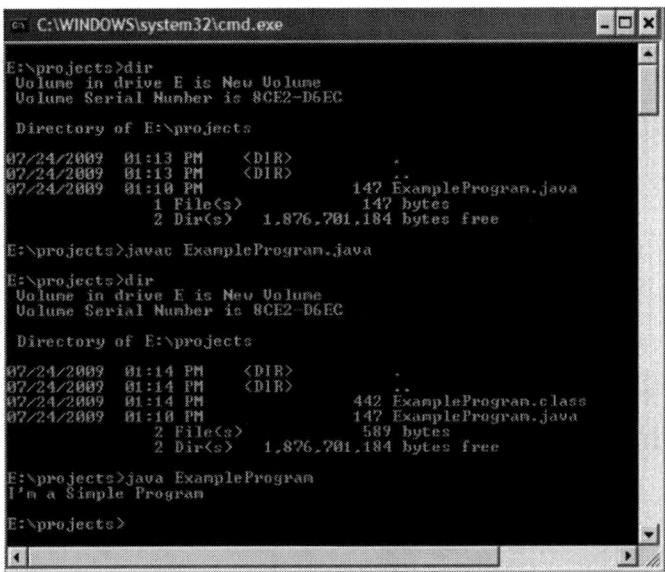

To run the program you just compiled, you will need to launch the *JVM*, which can be run from the command line by typing *java* followed by the name of your compiled *class* file (without the .class extension):

```
java ExampleProgram
```

Here is the same sequence in a Mac terminal window:

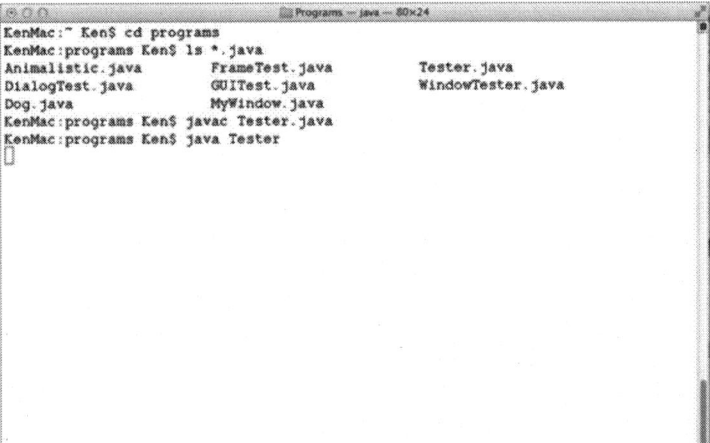

So that's all there is to creating, compiling, and running a Java program. Back to the layers we learned about earlier, the *ExampeProgram.java* file was compiled to create an *ExampleProgram.class* file. That file was opened and managed by the Java Virtual Machine, which translated it for the host operating system. Additional layers we didn't learn about are below the operating system. The operating system transforms requests from the JVM into machine language, which is (finally!) down to a language that our CPU and the rest of our computer hardware can understand.

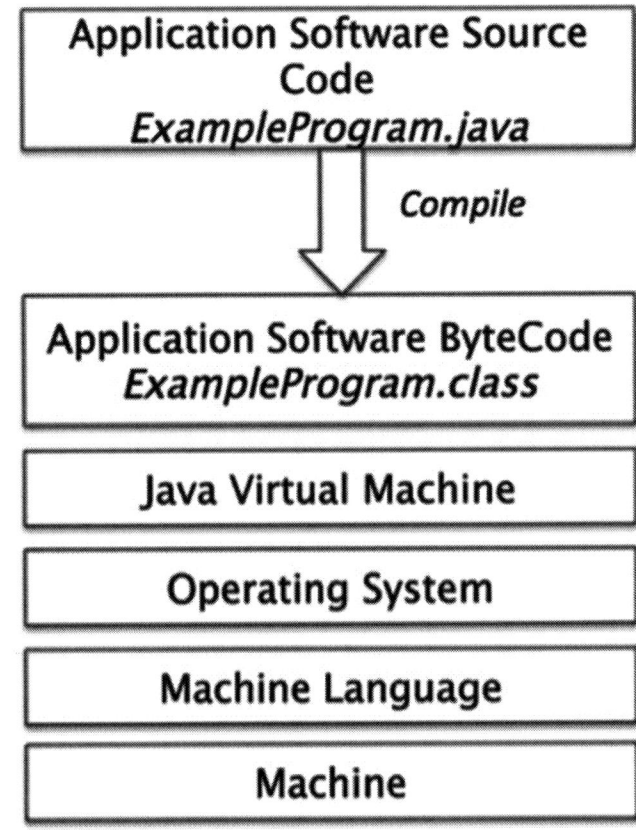

All these layers may seem inefficient, but they save us a lot of effort and cost by allowing us to write software that's usable on multiple platforms. The communication between the layers is so fast with today's modern computer technology, that overhead from multiple layer-to-layer communication is hardly noticeable.

Next we'll start to learn the syntax of the Java programming language so we can make our programs do interesting things.

PROGRAM FUNDAMENTALS

THE CLASS SIGNATURE

The bare minimum code required to successfully compile a Java program is the following:

```
class ClassName { }
```

Although this program will compile, it doesn't contain any logic, so it won't do anything.

The word *class* is one of 50 reserved keywords in the Java programming language. It always precedes a class name (of our choosing) when creating a Java program. The class signature must always be followed by a set of curly braces. The curly braces represent a *block* which will contain the entire contents of the class.

It is conventional to declare most classes as *public* (another keyword) so that the class can be used by other classes. The *public* keyword precedes the keyword *class*:

```
public class ClassName { }
```

THE MAIN METHOD

All program logic must be contained inside what's referred to as a *method*, and each *method* must be contained inside the *block* of a *class*. Again, a *block* is a section of code that belongs together that is surrounded by a set of curly braces { and }. A *class* must have a corresponding *block*, and a *method* must have a *block* as well. We can also use additional *block*s inside a method's *block*, which we'll learn later.

A computer program could have many classes and many methods, but at a minimum it must have one class, and it must have a method named *main*. The *main* method is always the starting point whenever we launch a program we have written.

We will dissect the components of the *main* method signature later. For now, just create a *main* method with the signature below inside the class's block (curly braces):

```
public class ClassName
    {
        public static void main(String[] args)
        {
        //program logic will go here
        }
    } //end class
```

COMMENTS

Comments are notes you include in your program that are intended to remind you what you did, or to help explain something to someone else who looks at your program. They are ignored by the Java compiler.

Any text that begins with a double slash // is considered a comment, and will be ignored by the compiler. Everything from the // symbols until the end of the line will be ignored, but the text that precedes the // symbols will still be compiled and executed.

A multi-line comment block can be created without having to put // at the beginning of every line. Any text surrounded by /* and */ will be considered a comment, even if it spans multiple lines.

```
//This entire line is a comment
System.out.println("Text"); //This print statement will compile, but the
                            //rest of the (and this line too) will
                            //be skipped by the compiler
/* Everything typed here
and here,
and here
until the closing comment symbol will be ignored by the compiler */
```

WHITE SPACE

The Java compiler ignores extra white space, so feel free to organize your program code in whatever format you like. For example, you can indent lines and match up your curly braces vertically, or you could scrunch everything together on a single line. The compiler won't care. (Others who look at your program might care though!)

The following two programs will compile and work identically:

```
public class MyClass {public static void main(String[] args){System.out.
print("X");}}
```

```
public class MyClass
    {
        public static void main(String[] args)
        {
            System.out.print("X");
        }
    }
```

IDENTIFIER NAME RULES AND CONVENTIONS

When naming a class, there are certain naming rules that the compiler requires, and other naming conventions that Java programmers typically follow. These same conventions will also be used for naming methods and variables. We refer to the name of a class, method or variable as an *identifier*.

First, the rules:

- An identifier may contain letters, digits, underscores _ or dollar signs $
- An identifier may not contain any spaces
- An identifier may not begin with a digit (it must be a letter, _ or $)

Now the conventions:

- Capitalize every word in the name of a class
- Capitalize all except the first word in the name of a method or variable

Sample class names:

```
ThisIsMyClass
AnotherClass
```

Sample method or variable names:

```
runThisMethod
thisIsAVariableName
```

PRINTING

When running a program, we frequently need to display output such as an informational message, a prompt to ask the user to enter something on the keyboard, or the output value from performing a calculation. Later in the book we'll learn how to build graphical user interfaces to display information. For now, we will use the console (Mac terminal or Windows CMD window) to display output. There are multiple ways to print information on the console. The first of these is the *println* statement:

```
System.out.println("some text");
```

The first part of this expression, *System.out* represents the standard Java output destination, which by default is the terminal or cmd window. When using a Java development environment like Eclipse, the tool intercepts *System.out* messages and displays output in its own console window.

The next part of the expression is *println*, which is called "print line." The *println* portion of the expression is a method that contains the actual logic that does the printing. It, like all methods, includes a set of parenthese after the method name. Inside the parentheses, a text string is passed to it.

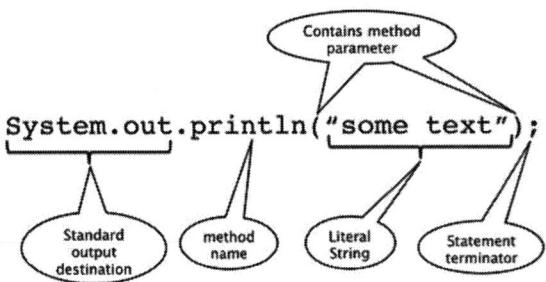

The text string inside the parentheses is any text contained inside a set of double quotes. This is referred to as a *literal String*. Note that *String* is capitalized. This is because a *String* is a specific declared type of data in Java. We'll learn more about data types later.

The final part of the expression is easily overlooked—the semicolon. The ; symbol is a statement terminator in Java, and is required at the end of each Java statement. We didn't include semicolons in our class or method blocks, because they aren't Java statements. A Java statement is one of the lines of code contained inside the block of a method.

ANOTHER PRINT STATEMENT

Now that we know how to use *println*, let's try another print statement:

```
System.out.print("some text");
```

The only syntax difference with this statement is the removal of the "ln" at the end of the method name. The difference when running these is where the printing "pointer," referred to as the cursor, is located after the print statement.

When a *println* message is sent, the cursor is automatically placed at the beginning of the next line. When a *print* message is sent, however, the cursor remains at the spot where it left off.

So the following three lines:

```
System.out.println("one");
System.out.println("two");
System.out.println("three");
```

Would generate the following output on the console:

```
one
two
three
```

If we change these to *print* statements, however:

```
System.out.print("one");
System.out.print("two");
System.out.print("three");
```

The output would be:

```
onetwothree
```

Which should we use? It depends what we want the output to look like. If we want each value to print on a separate line, *println* is convenient. If we want to control when a *newline* occurs, we should use *print*.

If we want to force a *newline* to occur (moving the cursor to the beginning of the next line) we can include the *escape sequence \n* inside our *String*. Whenever the \n two-character sequence is encountered inside a literal *String*, either a *print* or *println* statement will automatically move the cursor to the beginning of the next line at that point, then it will continue printing the rest of the content.

So, if we change our *print* statements as follows:

```
System.out.print("one");
System.out.print("two\n");
System.out.print("three");
```

The output would be:

```
onetwo
three
```

ONE MORE PRINT STATEMENT – *PRINTF*

So *print* and *println* offer two ways to display text on the console window. They are slightly different. Basically, *println* is just a *print* statement with a "\n" automatically stuck on the end of it.

Next we'll learn about a third print statement that offers more functionality: the *printf* statement.

The base form of the *printf* statement works the same way as the *print* statement. It prints a *String* passed in as its parameter, and leaves the cursor on the same line at the end of that *String*:

```
System.out.printf("some text");
```

The *String* in a *printf* statement can also include substitution symbols that are replaced with values at the time the program is run. The substitution symbols are placed within the *String*, and the values to be substituted are contained within the *printf*'s parentheses following the *String*. Each value is separated by a comma. For each substitution symbol contained inside the *String*, there must be a corresponding parameter with a value of that type following the *String*:

Substitution of one *String* using **%s**:

```
System.out.printf("Four score and %s years ago", "seven");
```

Substitution of an integer using **%d**:

```
System.out.printf("Four score and %d years ago", 7);
```

Substitution of a floating point number using **%f**:

```
System.outprintf("The value of pi is approximately %f", 3.1415);
```

Example with multiple substitution values in the same statement:

```
System.out.printf("String: %s Integer: %d Double: %f\n","text", 5, 3.1415);
```

The output from running this statement will be:

```
String: text Integer: 5 Double: 3.141500
```

Notice how extra zeros were padded on the end of the floating point number. By default, *printf* will automatically limit (and force) the display of a floating point number to have six digits to the right of a decimal point. You can override the default by inserting a width specifier and a precision specifier between the % and the f.

- Using a width specifier of 20 will force the output to occupy a width of 20 spaces. If the number requires fewer than 20 spaces, the output will be padded in front of the number.
- Using a precision specifier of .2 will round the floating point number to the hundredths value on the right of the decimal point.
- Combining these width and precision values would look like this %15.2f:

```
System.out.printf("$%15.2f", 12345.67890);
```

Would display:

```
$   12345.68
```

The width specifier pertains to the number. In the example, the $ is displayed followed by the 15 character wide formatted number. The table below depicts the character count:

$							1	2	3	4	5	.	6	8
	1	2	3	4	5	6	7	8	9	10	11	12	13	14	15

The purpose of these formatting symbols is to create structured output that displays information in nicely formatted columns.

The width specifier can also be used with integers and strings. For example,

```
System.out.printf("$%5dxx%10s",1,"is one");
```

Would display:

```
$    1xx    is one
```

$					1	X	X				I	S		O	N	E
	1	2	3	4	5			1	2	3	4	5	6	7	8	9	10

When the width specifier exceeds the size of the *String*, integer or floating point number, the displayed output will be right justified within that space and stuffed with blank spaces to the left. To left justify the output, put a minus sign (-) in front of the width specifier. Also, include a comma (,) with a floating point number will put a comma at each thousandths point on the left of the decimal.

The following diagram depicts a statement with these formatting elements, along with a column by column breakdown of the output:

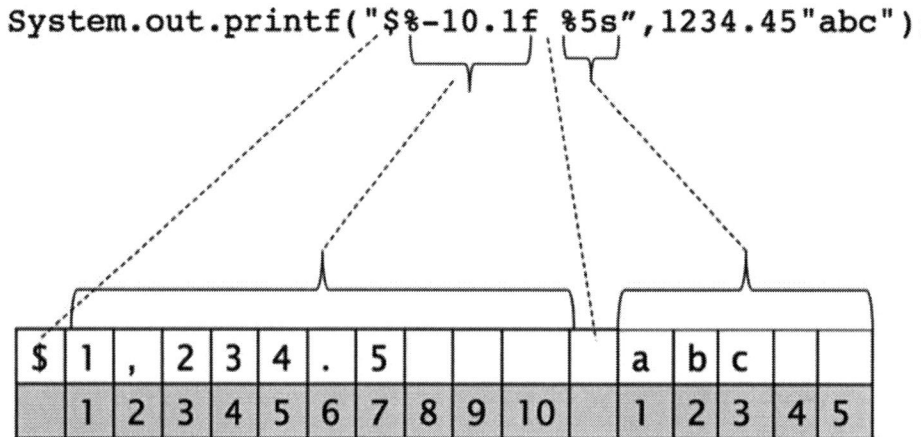

A summary of the *printf* substitution symbols:

% S	STRING
%S	String converted to all CAPS
%d	Integer
%nd	Integer filled (right justified) to width of n spaces
%-nd	Integer filled (left justified) to width of n spaces
%f	Floating point number (double or float)
%n.mf	Floating point number (right justified) to width of n spaces and rounded to m values on the right of the decimal
%,n.mf	Same as previous, adding comma at every thousandths
%-,n.mf	Same as previous, left justified

VARIABLES

When performing functions in a computer program, we often need to retain some data values for use later in the calculation. You did a lot this when you learned algebra, in problems like this:

```
x = y + 5;
if y = 10, what is the value of x?
```

We will make frequent use of variables in our Java programs. The names we give our variables can be simple letters like x, y, and z as shown above. They can also be given longer meaningful names such as myAge, yearOfBirth, etc. They just need to follow the identifier naming rules described earlier in this chapter.

Java is a *strongly typed* language, which means that before we can use a new variable in our program, we must declare its type. In other words, we must let the compiler know what type of data we plan to put in this variable. The reason this is required is to manage the memory resources of our computer efficiently. When a variable is declared, a portion of the main memory of our computer (RAM) will be set aside and dedicated to that variable. In the illustration below, variables x and y are declared as integers (int) within a block. Although x and y don't have values assigned to them yet, they are available for use in other statements within the same block.

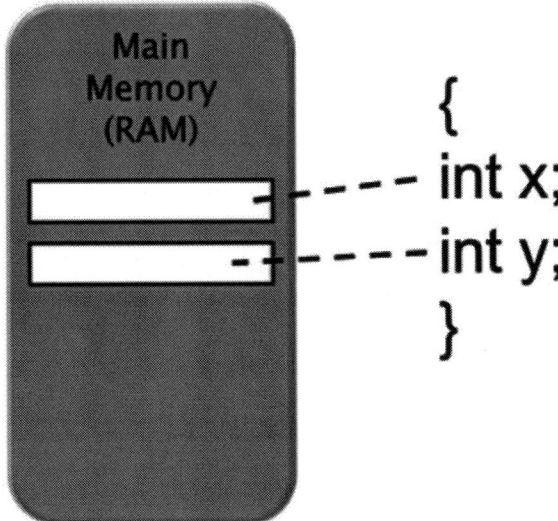

Adding two statements to the block: x = 5 and y = x + 2, will utilize these allocated memory spaces to store and retrieve integer values. In the illustration below, the statement *x = 5* causes the integer 5 to be put in *x*'s memory location. In the next statement x's value is retrieved, 2 is added to it, and the result is stored in y's memory address:

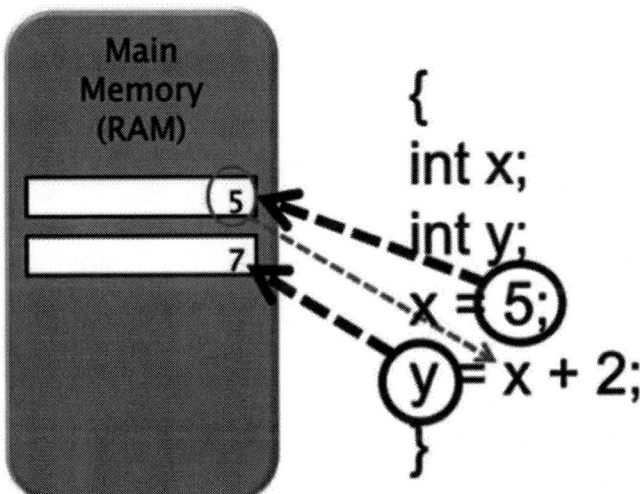

When a variable is declared of a specified type, we cannot use that variable for any other type of data. For example, the following would not compile:

```
int x = 5.5;
```

A variable declared as an *int* can only be used to hold integer values. Java includes eight primitive types that can be used to declare variables. Some of these will be used more than others.

INTEGERS

There are three primitive types that are used four integers: *short*, *int*, and *long*. The difference between these types is the amount of memory each one is allocated. The type *short* is used for small numbers in the range of -32,767 to +32,767. An *int* can hold values in the range of (approximately) -2.1 billion to +2.1 billion. A *long* holds values in the range of $\pm 2^{63}$.

Since the *long* type is the most flexible, why not declare everything as a *long?* We don't do this because *long* variables are allocated a lot more memory than *short*s and *int*s. We would be hogging up a lot of unnecessary memory. Since computers have a limited amount of memory, it's best to only reserve the amount of memory that we'll truly need.

It's customary to use *int* as our default choice when declaring an integer variable. Also, when a number without a decimal point is typed as a literal value in a program, Java treats it as an int.

FLOATING POINT NUMBERS

There are two primitive types for floating point numbers: *float* and *double*. A *float* reserves less memory than a *double*, and will truncate its value due to the memory restriction. This could cause problems with some calculations because even very small numbers could have a great number of digits to the right of the decimal point. For this reason, the default choice for floating point numbers is the more precise *double*. Also, when a literal numeric value that includes a decimal point is typed in a program, Java treats it by default as a *double*.

OTHER PRIMITIVE TYPES

In additional the five number primitive types, there are three additional primitive types that can be used to declare variables in Java:

PRIMITIVE TYPE	USAGE
char	A character
byte	A byte
boolean	true or false

STRING

In addition to the eight primitive types, there are countless other possible types in Java. Some are included with the language, others we can actually create ourselves. We'll learn more about that in a later chapter.

We have previously referenced strings several times. A *String* is actually a Java type than can be used to declare variables that will be used for storing text values. A literal *String* is any text typed into your program that is surrounded by a set of double quotes, such as:

```
String myString = "four score and seven years ago";
```

Note that the type *String* is capitalized, but the eight primitive types are not capitalized (*int, short, long, float, double, char, byte, boolean.*)

MATH OPERATORS

Java supports the following math operators:

MATH OPERATION	JAVA MATH OPERATOR	EXAMPLE
Addition	+	x + 7
Subtraction	-	x − y
Multiplication	*	x * y
Division	/	x / y
Remainder	%	x % 2
Assignment	=	x = y + 2

These math operators work with literal numerical values, or variables that have been declared as one of the five number primitive types. When using a numeric variable in a math expression, the variable must not only be declared, but it must also contain a value.

We use the assignment operator = to put a value in a variable. Everything to the right of an assignment operator will fully resolve to a single value, then that value will be stored in the variable to the left of the assignment operator.

The standard math operators for addition, subtraction, multiplication, and division are self-explanatory. Note that there are no implicit math operations, though. For example, in Algebra the expression xy is treated as x times y. This doesn't work in Java. To multiply x times y you must include the * multiplication operator: x * y.

One math operator that is not as commonly known is the mod function, which uses operator %. With mod, the value on the left is divided by the value on the right, and the result is the remainder. The result of 5 % 2 is 1 (2 goes into 5 twice, with a remainder of 1. The result of 5%3 is 2 (3 goes into 5 once with a remainder of 2.

ORDER OF OPERATIONS

Java follows the standard algebraic order of evaluation (precedence) when evaluating a math expression:

1st	* / and % are evaluated from left to right
2nd	+ and − are evaluated from left to right
3rd	= is evaluated last

Any portion of the expression contained is resolved ahead of elements outside the parentheses. The order of operations above is adhered to within the parentheses.

Examples:

JAVA EXPRESSION	VALUE OF X
int x = 2 + 2;	4
int x = 5 % (3 − 1) ;	1
int x = 10 + 10 / 2;	15
int x = (10 + 10) * 2;	40

BOOLEAN EXPRESSIONS

A boolean refers to the value *true* or *false*. One of the Java primitives *boolean* is used to hold a boolean value. We will need boolean values when including conditional expressions in programs—statements that only execute if a certain condition is true.

Boolean values are determined using the following operators:

OPERATOR	DESCRIPTION
>	Is greater than
<	Is less than
>=	Is greater than or equal to
<=	Is less than or equal to
==	Is equal to
!=	Is not equal to

The following expressions calculate a boolean value and store the result in the variables x and y that have been declared as booleans:

```
boolean x = 5 < 10; // will assign the value true to variable x

boolean y= 5 > 10 // will assign the value true to variable y
```

Note that the value *true* and the value *false* are Java keywords that are reserved to represent these two boolean values. These words can be included as literal values within a Java statement.

SIMPLE CONDITIONAL STATEMENT

By itself, a boolean value has little value. It is usually used to construct a conditional Java statement – one that executions only if a certain condition is true. The simplest conditional statement has the following structure:

```
if(boolean-expression)
Java statement; //Only executes if boolean-expression is true
```

An example:

```
int a = 10;
int b = 20;
if(a < b)
System.out.println("%d is less than %d", a, b);
```

We'll look at more things we can do with the *if* statement in the next chapter.

KEYBOARD INPUT

Most of the programs we have built so far include numeric data, and to this point we have "hard coded" the data values in our program. This means that the program has statements that assign variables to specific values.

What if we don't want to hard code data values in our program? How can we prompt a user of our program to enter a data value when the program is running? One way to do this is with the library class *Scanner*.

The class *Scanner* is a utilitarian class that is part of the Java development kit (JDK.) When you install the JDK on your computer, over 4000 library classes are included that you can use in your program. These classes provide a lot of functionality that you don't have to build from scratch. Experienced programmers become familiar with the Java class libraries and reuse as much as possible when building new systems.

Because there are so many library classes, when you include one in your program you must tell the compiler where to find it. We do this with an *import* statement. The *import* statement is placed above the class signature. To import *Scanner*, we need to use *Scanner's* complete name including the location of its library:

```
import java.util.Scanner;
public class MyClass { .... (etc)
```

If you attempt to use a library class without importing it, your program won't compile. (There is one exception to this—library classes in the package *java.lang* are always automatically imported, so these classes do not require you to include an import statement.)

After importing the *Scanner*, we need to create a *Scanner* object inside the *main* method. We'll learn more about creating objects later. For now, just include the following code inside the *main* method. Remember that Java is case sensitive, so type it exactly as shown below:

```
Scanner input = new Scanner(System.in);
```

Next, we can include statements to will pause execution of your program and wait for the user of your program to enter a value on the keyboard. There is a different statement for each type of data we want to capture:

```
nextInt()    //Captures a primitive integer
nextDouble() //Captures a primitive double
nextLine()   //Captures everything typed as a String including spaces
next()       //Captures text typed up to the first space as a String
```

These *next* messages are used with the name we gave the Scanner (in this example, we named the *Scanner* "input." To capture an integer from the Scanner and store the result in variable x, we would include the following statement:

```
int x = input.nextInt();
```

As soon as an *input.next...* statement is encountered, the cursor will blink and wait for the user to enter a value. It's helpful to use a *print* statement prior to prompting for input to tell the user what they are being asked to enter:

```
System.out.print("Enter your age: ");
int age = input.nextInt();
```

The following complete example program prompts the user for a name and age, and prints out what was entered:

```java
import java.util.Scanner;
  public class Sample
  {
        public static void main(String[] args)
        {
        Scanner input = new Scanner(System.in);
        System.out.print("What is your name? ");
        String name = input.nextLine();
        System.out.println(); //print a blank line
        System.out.print("How old are you? ");
        int age = input.nextInt();
        System.out.printf("\nHello %s, you are %d years old\n",name,age);
        }//end main
  }//end class Sample
```

CHAPTER 3

CONTROL STATEMENTS

In the first chapter we learned how simple algorithms could be solved with Java. With the Java syntax we've learned so far, though, our algorithms must be very basic. For more complex algorithms, more language constructs will be required. In this chapter we'll learn how to create control statements in Java that offer us the ability to create more complex systems.

PSEUDOCODE

When presented with a problem that you want to solve using a Java program, jumping straight to programming could become complicated and confusing, especially for someone who is new to Java. A useful strategy to begin solving a problem is to write out the steps of the solution in plain narrative form. This is called pseudocode. Pseudocode doesn't map to a precise syntax of any programming language. Rather, it expresses the solution in a step-by-step form that is understandable by non-programmers, and could later be mapped to Java code.

For example, let's evaluate the following problem:

A teacher wants to capture the numeric score that each student received on an exam, and summarize the results to determine how what percent of students in the class received a grade of A, B, C, D, and F.

Without jumping into a Java solution, let's describe the solution using pseudocode. Treat this exercise as though you were giving step-by-step instructions to the teacher to perform these steps manually:

```
Set counters for ACounter, BCounter,CCounter,DCounter and FCounter to zero
Set studentCount to 0
Prompt user to enter the grade of one student (or -1 to stop)
        increment studentCount by 1
        if grade is greater than or equal to 90, increment ACounter by 1
        if grade is between 80 and 89, increment BCounter by 1
        if grade is between 70 and 79, increment CCounter by 1
        if grade is between 60 and 69, increment DCounter by 1
        if grade is below 60, increment FCounter by 1
Repeat for the next student until -1 is entered
Using studentCount and ACounter, calculate APercent

Using studentCount and BCounter, calculate BPercent
Using studentCount and CCounter, calculate CPercent
Using studentCount and DCounter, calculate DPercent
Using studentCount and FCounter, calculate FPercent
Print (with labels) the values of APercent through FPercent
```

As you can see in this example, there is no compilable Java syntax. We simply describe the steps in a methodical way. To implement this in Java, there are some Java language elements that we'll need to learn:

```
Mixing data types (int and double) in one expression
Incrementers and decrementers
```

```
Selection control statements
Repetition control statements
```

We will develop a solution to this grade counter problem later in the chapter after we've learned these language elements.

MIXING DATA TYPES

In the last chapter we learned that Java is very picky about data types so it can manage the use of the computer's memory very rigorously. For this same reason, we must pay careful attention when mixing data types in the same Java statement.

If the following three lines were included in a Java program, what would be the value of z:

```
int x = 5000000;
int y = 1000;
int z = x * y;
```

At first glance it appears that z would have the value 5 billion (5 million times 1000.) However, there are two rules that Java follows when evaluating code that would give us the wrong result when running this program:

1. A literal numeric value that doesn't contain a decimal point is always treated as an int.
2. An int times an int always gives an int result.
3. An int has a size limit of approximately ± 2.15 billion.
4. The assignment operator is always executed last, after everything to the right of it has completely resolved to a single value.

Because of these rules, the literal value 5000000 times the literal value 1000 are treated as an int times an int, and the result will be treated as an int. An int cannot contain the number 5000000000 because it's too large to fit into an int, so the program result will be inaccurate. This will not cause a compile error nor will it display an error at runtime. It will just stuff an incorrect (incomplete calculation) value in the variable z.

You might be inclined to fix this by declaring z as a *long*, because *long*s can store very large numbers:

```
int x = 5000000;
int y = 1000;
long z = x * y;
```

This won't solve the problem, however, because x and y are both *ints,* and the calculation on the right of the equal sign will still resolve to an *int* result before the assignment to z occurs. Even though z is a *long,* we had an incorrect result before the assignment to z happened.

The only way to get an accurate calculation on the right side of the expression is for one or both of the values to be *long*s. A non-floating point number can be treated as a *long* instead of an *int* by putting the suffix L at the tail end of the number. This will multiply the *long* x times the *int* y, yielding a *long* result that is stored in *long* z.

```
long x = 5000000L;
int y = 1000;
long z = x * y;
```

We run into a similar problem when mixing integers with floating point numbers. The following statements will not result in a compile or runtime error, but the result will be inaccurate:

```
int x = 5;
int y = 2;
int z = x / y;
```

Because and *int* divided by an *int* will always give us an *int* result, diving 5 by 2 will result in z containing the value 2. Java truncates everything to the right of the decimal place when stuffing a floating point number into an *int*.

The only way to overcome this problem is to make sure either the numerator or the denominator of the division expression is a *double*. A *double* divided by an *int* (or an *int* divided by a *double*) with give a *double* result.

By changing x to a double, and also changing z do a double to contain the result of the calculation, we eliminated the loss of precision problem:

```
double x = 5;
int y = 2;
double z = x / y;
```

CASTING

When mixing data types we may not want to change the data type just to make a division equation work properly. In the previous example, we are consuming a lot more memory by making x a double. Since it only contains the value 5, we don't really need the additional space allocated to it to store decimal values. In a case like this, we can temporarily change x to a double for a single equation, then it will resume to be an *int* after execution of the equation.

To accomplish this, we temporarily promote the variable x to a double by putting *(double)* in front of x at the place where we need to promotion to occur. This is called *casting*:

```
int x = 5;
int y = 2;
double z = (double) x / y;
```

It's not necessary to promote both x and y in this example, because either the numerator or the denominator must be promoted, but not both. Because the result of this division expression will be a double, make sure that result is stored in a *double* variable. In this case, we declare z as a double.

⏣ COMPOUND ASSIGNMENT OPERATORS

The use of an *int* variable as a counter is commonly used in programming. Assuming we already have a variable named c that is declared as an *int* and has been assigned to some valid integer value, the following statement could be used to add 3 to c's current value:

```
c = c + 3;
```

If c's previous value was 2, it would now contain the value 5. It basically takes c's previous value and adds 3 to it.

We will frequently use statements like this to keep track of a counter when repeating a set of Java statements a specified number of times. We will learn more about this later in the chapter.

There is also a shortcut version of this expression:

```
c += 3; //means the same thing as c = c + 3
```

We can use this shortcut, which is referred to as a *compound assignment operator* with the math operators +, -, *, / and %.

OPERATION	FULL STATEMENT	COMPOUND STATEMENT
Addition	x = x + 5;	x += 5;
Subtraction	x = x -5;	x -= 5;
Multiplication	x = x * 5;	x *= 5;
Division	x = x / 5;	x /= 5;
Mod	x = x % 5;	x %= 5;

INCREMENTERS/DECREMENTERS

When incrementing or decrementing an integer by one, there is another shortcut that is commonly used in Java programming: The incrementor and decrementor operators. Each of these can be used as a standalone Java statement on a line by itself, or as part of a more complex Java statement:

```
x++;
++x;
x--;
--x;
```

The increment or decrement operators can be put in front or in back of the variable name that is to be changed. When these are on a line by themselves, it doesn't matter whether the prefix or postfix version is used.

However, when the incrementing or decrementing is occurring as part of a bigger expression, it's important to understand when the incrementing (or decrementing) will occur:

- With prefix versions (++x or --x) the incrementing/decrementing occurs before anything else on that line of Java code is evaluated.
- With postfix versions (x++ or x--) the incrementing/decrementing occurs after everything else on the line of Java code is evaluated *including the assignment operation*.

Let's look at an example and evaluate what occurs during each line of code:

```
int x = 1;    //x is declared as an int and assigned value 1
int y = 2;    //y is declared as an int and assigned value 2
int z = x++;  //z is declared as an int and assigned value 1
              //After assigning 1 to z, x is incremented to 2
z = x + --y   //The value of y is decremented to 1, then z is
              //assigned the value of x (1) plus y (1), or 2
```

CONTROL STRUCTURES

Java statements execute by default in sequential order from the first line of the *main* method until the closing curly brace is encountered. This is referred to as *sequential execution*. Often, we need to need to specify variations to sequential execution:

Selection Statements: Used to execute specified Java statements if a certain condition is true or false. These are implemented using *if, if...else,* or *switch* statements.

Repetition Statements: Used to repeat a line or block of code. Loops will continue to repeat execution as long as some boolean expression continues to evaluate to *true*. It exits when the condition becomes *false*. Repetition statements are implemented using *while, do..while,* or *for* statements.

SELECTION CONTROL STATEMENT: *IF*

At the end of the previous chapter we introduced the *if* statement. The *if* statement requires a single parameter which is a boolean expression that evaluates to the value *true* or *false*. If the result of the expression is *true*, the statemen following the *if* will execute, otherwise it will be skipped.

```
int y = 10;
if (y > 2)
System.out.println("it is true"); //Executes only if y is greater than 2
System.out.println("end");        //always executes
```

The *if* statement is only tied to the next Java statement that follows it. In the example above, the "end" String will always print because it is not linked to the *if* statement.

If you want multiple lines of code to execute if the condition is true, use a *block* with the *if* statement that contains all the statements that are linked to the conditional expression:

```
int y = 10;
if (y > 2)
    {
    System.out.println("y is greater than 2");
    System.out.println("also print this only when the condition is true");
    }
System.out.println("always print this");
```

SELECTION CONTROL STATEMENT: *IF..ELSE*

When you have an either/or situation based on evaluation of a boolean expression, the *if..else* statement let's you specify behavior for both the *true* and for the *false* conditions:

```
int y = 10;
if (y > 2)
    System.out.println("y is greater than 2");
else
    System.out.println("y is not greater than 2");
```

Just like the simple *if* statement, a block of code could be used following the *if*, following the *else*, or following both. Without a block, only a single line of code is executed for the *if* and for the *else*.

```
int y = 10;
if (y > 2)
    {
    System.out.print("y IS ");
    System.out.println("greater than 2");
    }
else
    {
    System.out.print("y IS NOT ");
    System.out.println("greater than 2");
    }
```

NESTED SELECTION STATEMENTS

It's possible to include another *if* statement within another *if* or *else* block:

```
int y = 10;
if (y > 2)
    {
    System.out.println("y IS GREATER than 2");
    }
else
    {
        if(y == 2)
                System.out.println("y IS EQUAL to 2");
        else
                System.out.println("y IS LESS than 2");
    }
```

Because an *if..else* statement is treated as a single Java statement, the else block does not require the curly braces in the example above. This could appear to be confusing to those who are new to Java programming. If the curly braces help you better understand the organization and structure of your program, feel free to include them. Here is the previous example without curly braces, and with extraneous white space removed:

```
int y = 10;
if (y > 2) System.out.println("y IS GREATER than 2");
else if(y == 2) System.out.println("y IS EQUAL to 2");
else System.out.println("y IS LESS than 2");
```

SELECTION CONTROL STATEMENT: *SWITCH*

The *switch* statement is a convenient way to simplify a potentially complex series of nested *if..else* statements when testing a variable for multiple possible values. There are several elements to a properly formatted *switch* statement that must be handled:

- A variable that has been declared as a *byte*, *short*, *int*, or *char* and has been assigned to a value of that type.
- A *switch* statement with the variable above as its parameter
- A block containing *case*, *break*, and *default* statements.

Here is an example of a menu selection system. Read the inline comments for an explanation of what each statement does:

```
import java.util.Scanner; //to allow us to prompt the user for an int

public class Menu {
public static void main(String[] args) {
    Scanner input = new Scanner(System.in); //Allows for keyboard input
    //Display the menu to the user:
    System.out.println("MENU:";
    System.out.println(" 1. Print one";
    System.out.println(" 2. Print two";
    System.out.println(" 3. Print three";
    System.out.println(); //empty line
```

```
      System.out.print("Enter choice: "); //note the use of print, not println
      int x = input.nextInt(); //get an int from the keyboard

switch (x) //Will compare case statements against the value of x
{
   case 1:
         System.out.println("one");
         break; //without the break, subsequent lines will execute
   case 2:
         System.out.println("two");
         break;
   case 3:
         System.out.println("three");
   default:
         System.out.println("none of the above");
}//end switch
}//end main
}//end class
```

An important feature of a *switch* statement's behavior is that once a *case* statement is encountered that matches the value of the parameter of the *switch* statement, The remaining *case* statements will be ignored, and every subsequent line in the *switch* block will execute. A *break* statement, however, will cause execution to jump directly to the end of the *switch* block. For this reason, you will usually want to make sure you include a *break* statement at the end of each *case* section.

If none of the *case* statements match, none of the statements in the *switch* statement will execute. You may add an optional *default* section that will execute if all other cases are false.

REPETITION CONTROL STATEMENT: *WHILE*

Another category of control statements represents those used to repeat execution of a block of code. The while statement will repeatedly evaluate the boolean expression contained in its parameter and will repeat its block of code until that expression becomes false. This means that the boolean expression should contain a variable, and that variable's value should change inside the *while* block so the boolean expression eventually becomes false.

```
int x = 10;
while(x < 100)
{
   System.out.print(x + " ");
   x = x + 10;
}
```

Executing this code should give the following output:

```
10 20 30 40 50 60 70 80 90
```

Each time x is incremented by 10, the loop returns to the while statement to evaluate the contents of x. As long as x continues to be less than 100, the block of code will repeat. After it prints 90, the value of x will be change to 100, then the while expression will evaluate the value of x one more time. Since 100 is not less than 100, the statement becomes false and it exits the while loop.

Just as with *if* statements, if there is only one line of code that repeats in the *while* block, the curly braces are optional. They are required, however, if more than one line of code is to be repeated.

Be cautious when using *while* loops to ensure that the false condition will eventually occur. The following code would result in an "endless loop" that will never end normally.:

```
int x = 10;
while(x < 100)
    x -= 10; //note the use of the compound assignment operator
```

When a program is stuck in a loop like this, you can force it to quit by pressing *control-c* on your keyboard.

COUNTER CONTROLLED REPETITION

A commonly used pattern with loops is called counter controlled repetition. An *int* variable is used as a counter that keeps track of the number of times the loop has executed. When the counter reaches the desired number of loops, the *while* loop is exited. There are three parts of this program that must be present for counter controlled repetition to work:

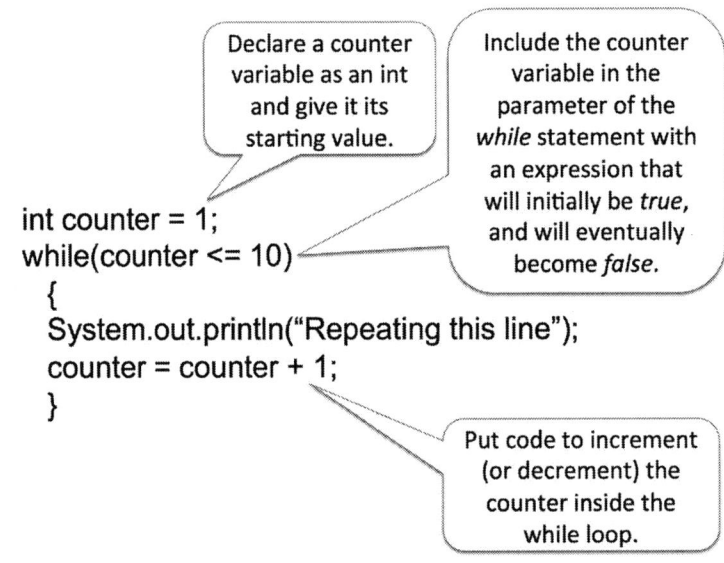

The counter can count upward or downward. Just make sure that you increment or decrement in the direction that will cause the boolean test to eventually become false. It's also not necessary to always count up or down in increments of one. The following loop prints all the event numbers between 2 and 50:

```
int counter = 2;
while(counter <= 50)
    {
        System.out.print( counter + " ");
        counter += 2;
    }
```

SENTINEL CONTROLLED REPETITION

Often we'll want to loop a block of code continuously until a user chooses to exit the loop. Since this requires user interaction with our program, we will need a Scanner object to capture keyboard input. When the user enters a predetermined exit value, which is referred to a sentinel value.

In the following loop, a user chooses options from a menu that is presented to them. This is the same menu we used for the switch statement earlier in the chapter. In this version, the menu will continue to print the value the user selects until the sentinel value (0) is selected:

```java
import java.util.Scanner; //to allow us to prompt the user for an int

public class Menu {
public static void main(String[] args) {
        Scanner input = new Scanner(System.in); //Allows for keyboard input
        int sentialValue = 99; //set the sentinel to a value that will be true
        while(sentinelValue != 0)
        {
        //Display the menu to the user:
        System.out.println("MENU:";
        System.out.println(" 1. Print one");
        System.out.println(" 2. Print two");
        System.out.println(" 3. Print three");
        System.out.println(" 0. EXIT");
        System.out.print("\nEnter choice: ");
        sentinelValue = input.nextInt(); //User enters new sentinelValue

        if(sentinelValue == 1) System.out.println("one");
        if(sentinelValue == 2) System.out.println("two");
        if(sentinelValue == 3) System.out.println("three");

        }//end while. Returns to while statement and checks for true/false
        }//end main
        }//end class
```

REPETITION CONTROL STATEMENT: *FOR*

The *for* statement is the most commonly used Java statement for managing loops. Everything you can do with a *while* loop can be done with a *for* statement. The *for* syntax is a bit more compact, so some feel that it is cleaner to look at. However, it's really a matter of preference which format you choose to use in your programs.

Syntax of the *for* statement:

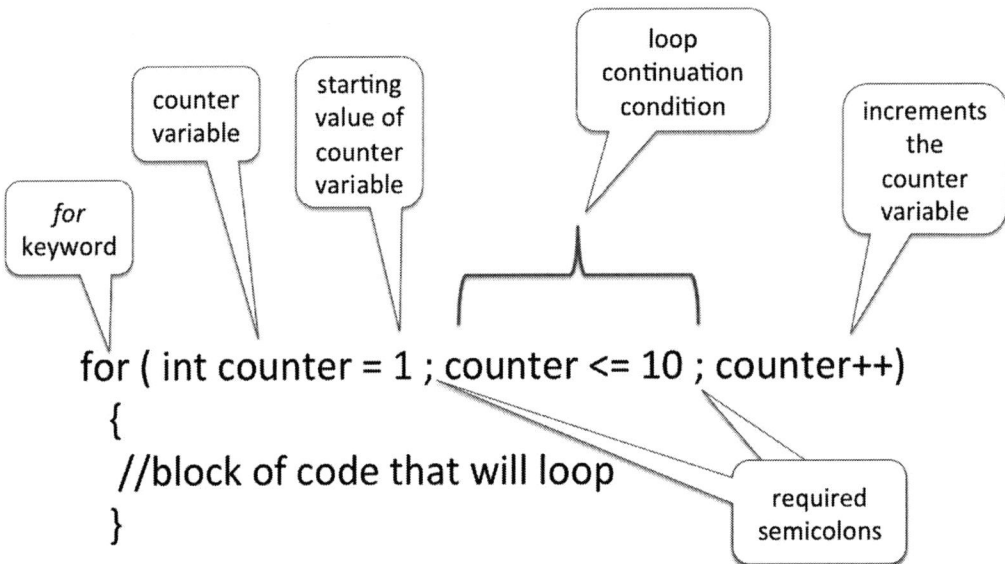

Note that everything in the *for* loop has a corresponding equivalent in the *while* loop. In the *while* loop the counter initialization, increment statement and continuation conditional test are on three separate lines, while they are all combined into one line in the *for* loop.

The contents of a *for* statement's parentheses is split into three sections. The semicolons separating the first and second sections as well as the second and third sections are required. However, the contents of each section are optional:

- The counter declaration and initialization could be omitted if these were done in a statement prior to the *for* loop.
- If the loop continuation condition is empty/blank, the condition is considered to be always *true*, which results in and endless loop.
- If the counter increment/decrement statement is missing, it could be handled within the block of the *for* loop.

The increment/decrement statement can be written using any of these formats:

```
counter = counter + 1
counter += 1
++counter
counter++
```

Also, the counter can increment or decrement by increments other than 1:

```
for (int i = 1; i < 100 ; i+=2) //counts up all odd numbers from 1 to 99,

for (int i = 100; i >= 1 ; i=i-5) //counts down from 100 to 5, by fives
```

As with *if* and *while* statements, the *for* loop does not require a set of curly braces unless more than one line will be contained in the block of code that will repeat. However, the curly braces can always be used even if there is only one statement that repeats.

```
for(int c = 100; c < 200; c+=25)
        System.out.print(c + "  "); //curly braces are optional

//generates output: 100 125 150 175
```

REPETITION CONTROL STATEMENT: *DO..WHILE*

The *do..while* statement is a variation of the *while* loop. The only difference between them is when the loop continuation condition is evaluated. With a regular *while* loop, the continuation test is performed at the beginning of the loop. Therefore, if the test is false at the beginning, the code inside the *while* loop's block will never execute.

With the *do..while*, the condition is tested at the end of the block. Therefore the looping code is guaranteed to always execute at least once. Here is an example:

```
int counter = 1;
do {
        System.out.print(counter + "  ");
        counter++;
    } while (counter < 5)
```

This will generate the following output:

```
1 2 3 4
```

The last time through the loop, 4 is printed, the counter is incremented to 5, then the continuation test determines that 5 is not less than 5, so it exits the loop at that point.

USING *BREAK* AND *CONTINUE* STATEMENTS

When using either counter controlled or sentinel controlled repetition, it's possible to interrupt the normal looping logic with *break* or *continue*. We saw *break* briefly when learning the *switch* statement. Now we'll learn a couple more ways to use it.

When a *break* statement is encountered, flow control moves automatically to the closing curly brace of the *while*, *for* or *switch* statement's block. The *break* statement is usually used as the result of a conditional (*if*) statement.

Example:

```
for( int counter = 1 ; counter <=10 ; counter++) {

if (counter == 5 )
  break; //exit the loop
System.out.print(counter + "  ");
}
//Prints: 1 2 3 4
//Exits the loop when 5 is encountered
```

You may find the *break* statement useful if you build a menu of choices that continues to display until the user chooses the "exit" option. When the "exit" option is selected you may want to bypass all remaining logic and exit out of the loop right away. A *break* statement will help you accomplish this.

A *continue* statement is like a soft *break*. When the *continue* statement is encountered, the remaining logic inside the loop's block is skipped, but it doesn't exit the loop. It will return to the top, evaluate the loop continuation condition, and continue to loop until the condition is met. Here is the previous example with *continue* instead of *break*:

```
for (int counter = 1 ; counter <=10 ; counter++) {
 if (counter == 5 )
      continue; //jump to the end of the loop, but don't exit
  System.out.print(counter + " ");
}
//Prints: 1 2 3 4 6 7 8 9 10
//skips the 5 due to the continue statement
```

LOGICAL OPERATORS

All of these selection and repetition control statements require boolean expressions to perform the conditional or continuation tests. In addition to the boolean operators we learned in the last chapter (<, >, <=, >=, ==, !=) there are additional logical operators that can be used to construct complex boolean expressions:

Logical operators are used to combine two boolean expressions and resolve them down to a single *true* or *false* result. The logical operators are:

LOGICAL OPERATORS	
&&	AND (with short circuiting)
&	AND (without short circuiting)
||	OR (with short circuiting)
|	OR (without short circuiting)
^	Logical exclusive OR
!	Logical NOT

The && operator ensures that both boolean expressions are *true*:

IF EXPRESSION A IS:	EXPRESSION B IS:	EXPRESSION A && EXPRESSION B
false	false	false
false	true	false
true	false	false
true	true	true

Example:

```
int x = 5;
int y = 10;
int z = 15;
if ( ( x < y ) && (y < z ) )
      System.out.println("all are in order");
```

When using &&, if the result of the first expression is *false*, the second expression is skipped and not evaluated. This is called *short circuiting*. When we learn that the first expression is *false*, we know that the result must be *false*, and it's not useful to evaluate the second expression.

If we desire the second expression to be evaluated anyway, we should use the single & operator, which bypasses short circuiting and evaluates the entire expression. This might be necessary if using incrementers/decrementers with variables in the second expression that we want to execute.

The || operator checks to see if either of the boolean expressions are *true*:

IF		
EXPRESSION A IS:	EXPRESSION B IS:	EXPRESSION A || EXPRESSION B
false	false	false
false	true	true
true	false	true
true	true	true

With the OR statement, short circuiting only happens when the first statement evaluates to *true*. If we want to bypass short circuiting and execute both expressions every time, the single | operator should be used for OR.

The ^ operator returns *true* if the expressions have opposing values—one is *true* and the other is *false*:

IF		
EXPRESSION A IS:	EXPRESSION B IS:	EXPRESSION A ^ EXPRESSION B
false	false	false
false	true	true
true	false	true
true	true	false

There is no short circuiting with this operator because both sides must always be evaluated to determine the result of the compound expression.

Finally, placing an exclamation mark (!) in front of any boolean expression automatically reverses its value: *true* becomes *false* and vice versa.

```
int x = 5;
int y = 10;
int z = 15;
if ( !( x > y ) && !(y > z ) )
        System.out.println("all are in order");
```

CHAPTER 4
METHODS

You have seen examples of Java code that forms the structure of a program such as *public class ExampleProgram* and *import java.util.Scanner.* Java statements that manage the flow and execute logic must exist within a *method*, and each *method* must be contained inside a *class*. Although it's possible to compile a *class* that doesn't contain any *methods*, that program can't actually do anything.

STATIC METHODS

A system may be comprised of one or more classes, and each of those classes may contain one or more methods. One of those classes must have a method named *main* because that is always the starting point for every system. The Java Virtual Machine (JVM) executes the *main* method, and flow control continues from there.

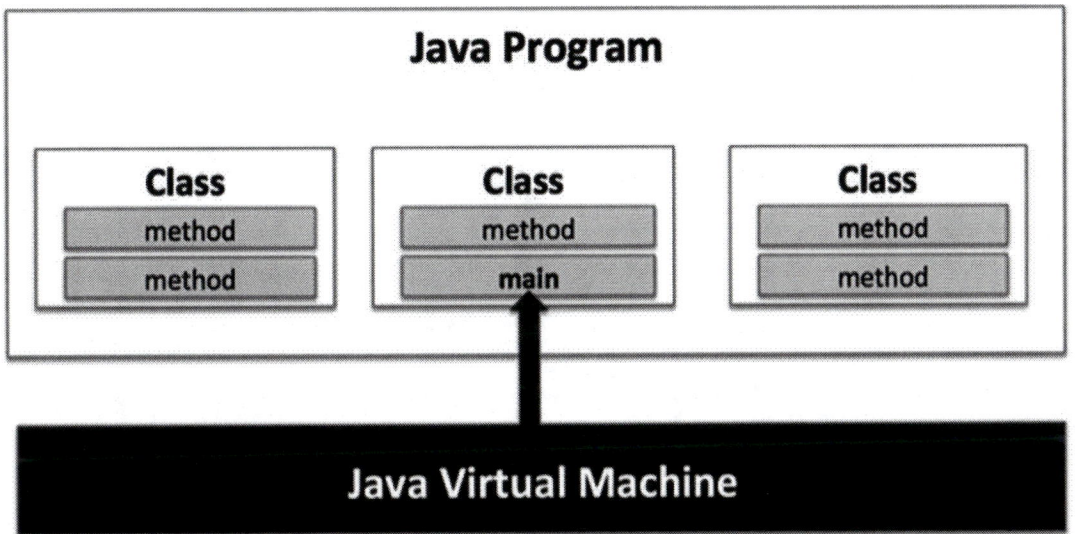

The *main* method is a *static* method, which means that it is invoked directly on the *class* itself. Later in the book we'll learn about object oriented programming, where methods are invoked in a different way. For now, though, we'll work strictly with static methods.

The statement "the *main* method is invoked directly on the *class* itself" means that when you run a program by passing a compiled *class* to the JVM, it implicitly invokes the following:

```
YourClassName.main();
```

REDUCING COMPLEXITY

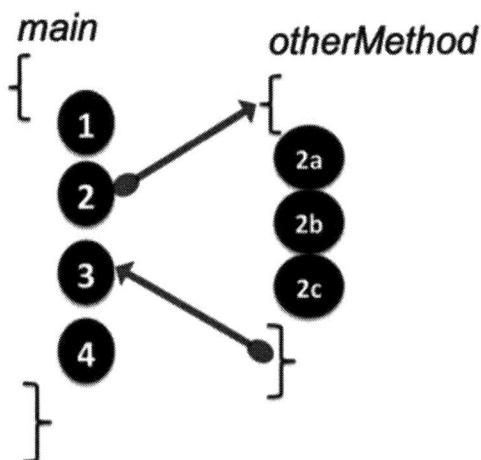

For small programs, a *main* method contained in a single class may be sufficient. However, when the *main* method starts to become big and complex, it can be broken up into multiple methods. When another method is called, flow control continues to be sequential, one step at a time. In the illustration to the right, step 2 in the *main* method invokes *otherMethod*. When *otherMethod* completes all of its steps, control resumes where it left off in the *main* method.

When a class contains multiple *static* methods, the methods can be called directly from within other methods in the same class. For example, if ClassA has methods *main*, *methodX* and *methodY*, the static methods can be invoked directly.

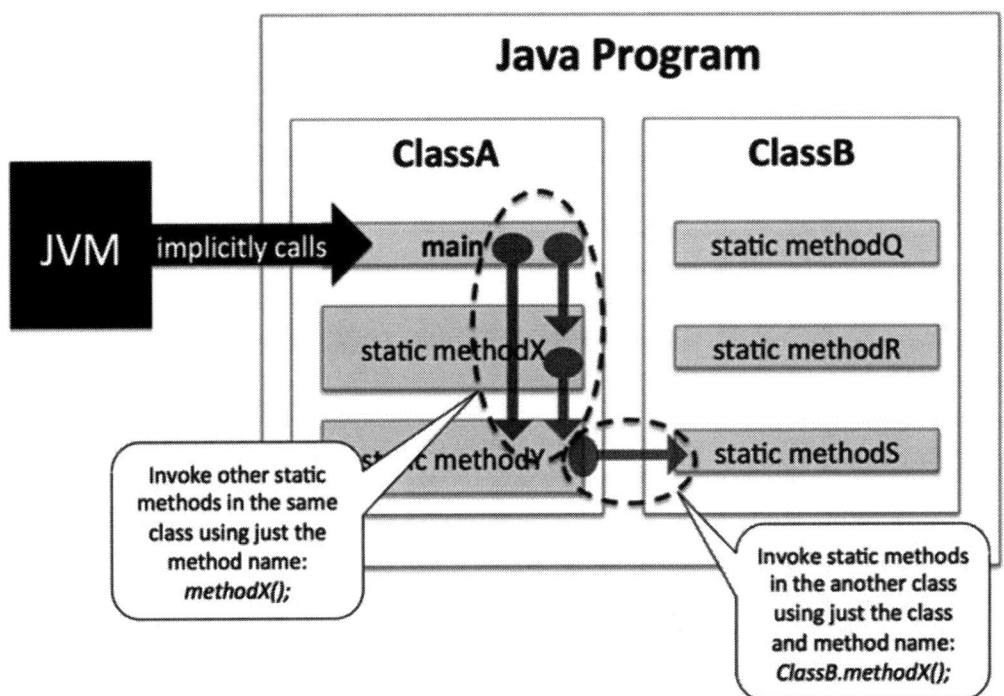

Here is an example of calling *methodX* and *methodY* from within *main*:

```java
public class ClassA {
  public static void main(String[] args)
  {
    System.out.println("in main");
    methodX();
    methodY();
    System.out.println("back in main");
  }
```

```
public static void methodX()
{
   System.out.println("in method X");
}

public static void methodY()
{
   System.out.println("in method Y");
}
} //end ClassA
```

If we want to execute *methodR* in *ClassB* from *ClassA*'s *main* method, however, we must include the method's class name:

```
public class ClassA {
   public static void main(String[] args)
   {
      System.out.println("in main");
      ClassB.methodR();
      methodX();
      methodY();
      System.out.println("back in main");
   }
}
```

etc...

USING METHODS IN LIBRARY CLASSES

Java comes bundled with over 4000 classes that are available to be used in programs that you build. One very useful class in the *java.lang* package is *Math*. The *Math* class contains several *static* methods that can be included in your programs. Since the *Math* class is contained in *java.lang*, it is imported automatically, and no *import* statement is required. All *static* methods in *Math* are invoked directly on the *Math* class using the format:

```
Math.methodName(parameters);
```

Using these methods can save you the trouble of building these commonly used algorithms from scratch. Some commonly used *Math* methods:

METHOD	DESCRIPTION
abs(x)	Absolute value of x
Math.ceil(x)	Round x to smallest integer not less than x
Math.cos(x)	Trigonometric cosine of x
Math.max(x,y)	Return larger of x and y
Math.min(x,y)	Return smaller value of x and y
Math.pow(x,y)	Raise x to the power of y
sqrt(x)	Square root of x

There are many more, but this provides a sampling. The following program demonstrates the use of one of these functions, *pow*:

```
public class MathTest {
public static void main(String[] args) {
        int x = 2;
        int y = 3;
        int z = Math.pow(2,3); //Assigns z to the result of 2 to the 3rd
power
}//end main
}//end class
```

STATIC FIELDS IN LIBRARY CLASSES

The *Math* class also includes some static fields that can be used in your programs. These are utilitarian data values that never change:

```
Math.PI //Contains the value of Pi
```

```
Math.E  //Contains the base value used in natural logarithms
```

DECLARING METHODS

When constructing a new method to include in your class (in addition to *main*) it should adhere to the following format:

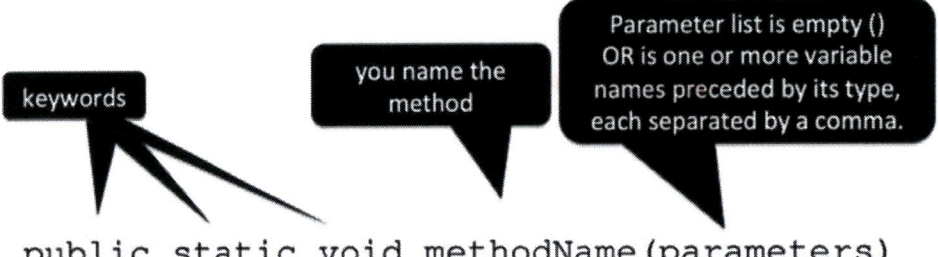

```
public static void methodName(parameters)
```

Examples (without method body content):

```
public static void doSomething() { }
```

```
public static void doThis( int x ) { }
```

```
public static void doThat( double d, String s) { }
```

Let's dissect the method signature one element at a time:

public	A public method can be invoked by other classes
static	Discussed earlier in the chapter
void	A Java keyword that indicates the method returns nothing. This will be replaced by a *type* indicator for methods that have a *return* statement (described later in the chapter)
methodName	Your choice, but it must adhere to the identifier naming rules and conventions.
parameters	Optional. If present, declares variables to contain data that is passed into the method to use in processing.

PARAMETERS

Parameters are optional in the method signature, although the parentheses are always required. If data is going to be passed to a method for processing, a variable must be declared to contain that data inside the parentheses of the method signature:

```
public static void myMethod(int x) //accepts an int passed into the method
```

The parameter variable (and its contents) can then be used anywhere inside the body of the method.

A method can accept multiple parameters. Each parameter must have a variable name preceded by its type (declaration.) Each of these type/variableName pairs must be separated by commas. Following is an example of a method with three parameters:

```
public static void doThis(int a, int b, String s)
```

METHOD BODY

Each method must have a block (set of curly braces) that contains its program logic. Just like the *main* method, each method will execute its statements from its beginning to its end.

All parameter variables in the method signature can be used within the method body. Also, new variables can be declared and used within the method body.

When it reaches the end of the block, program control resumes at the next statement in the method where this method was called. All the variables that were declared as parameters or inside the method body will no longer exist when the method reaches the closing curly brace. If the calling method needs data from this method, you must use a *return* statement.

THE *RETURN* STATEMENT

A method can optionally return something to the method that called it. If it does return something, it can only return one thing. Also, returning that piece of data must be the last line of the method. This is implemented using the return statement in this format:

```
return dataToBeReturned;
```

The *dataToBeReturned* can either be a literal value, or a variable that contains a value.

If a method has a *return* statement, the method signature must specify the type of the data being returned. This will replace the *void* keyword, which is used for methods that don't have a *return* statement.

Examples:

```java
public static int addTwo(int x)
{
  int y = x + 2; //adds 2 to the number passed in and stores it in y
  return y;   //returns the int contained in y
}

public static String tellMeSomething()
{
  return "Something!";   //returns the literal String "Something"
}
```

CALLING METHODS

A method within the same *class* is called (invoked) by including the method name (and its parameter values, if any) in a Java statement. The following *main* method includes statements that call the methods *addTwo* and *tellMeSomething* shown above:

```java
public static void main(String[]args)
{
int myVar = 12;

//Send the contents of variable myVar (12) to the addTwo method and
//put the result (14) in variable b
int b = addTwo(a);

//Call the tellMeSomething method, get the String it returns, and print
it
System.out.println(tellMeSomething());
}
```

VARIABLES AND METHODS

When working with multiple methods, it's important to remember that variables can only be used within the block (set of curly braces) where they are declared.

The illustration to the right depicts the scope of variables and blocks conceptually. The blocks could represent an *if* statement within a method, a *for* loop within a *while* loop, or any other configuration of a block within a block. In the example, note that the variable x is available in the outer and inner blocks because it can be used in any statement contained within the set of curly braces it was declared in. The variable *y*, however, has a narrower scope and cannot be used in the block outside where it was declared.

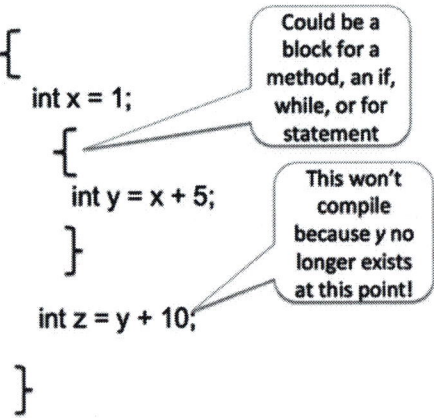

The scope of variables is subject to the same constraints when using multiple methods. Variables can only be used in the method where they are declared. When one method calls another method, each method can only use its own variables. There are only two ways to share data between methods:

1. Sending data as a parameter of the method. In this case, the data is passed, not the variable.

2. Returning data to the calling method with a *return* statement. Also in this case, the variable is not returned, just the data it contains.

The example below contains two methods. Execution always begins at the beginning of the *main* method. From that point, follow the sequence of execution and what happens with each variable and its value. The numbers indicate the sequence which things occur:

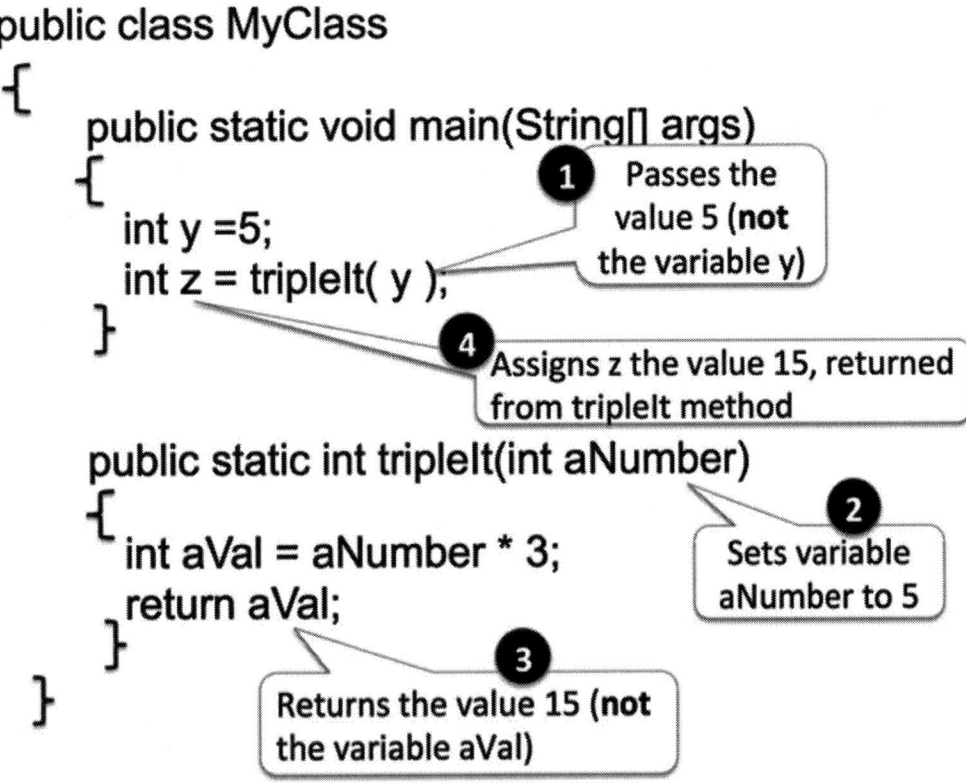

CASTING METHOD PARAMETERS

In the previous chapter we learned how to use *casting* to resolve issues with mixed data types. In one example, we temporarily promoted a variable containing an *int* to a *double* to perform division without loss of precision. After the math expression was complete, the variable resumed being an *int*.

We can also use casting with method parameters. This method accepts a *double* as a parameter:

```
public static void doSomething (double x)
{//method contents }
```

If we want tried to pass an int to this method, we wouldn't be able to compile our program. The compile error would be a "Data Type Mismatch." If our calling method has an *int* and we don't want to change that, we could call the *doSomething* method and cast the *int* value to a *double*, as shown here:

```
public static void main(String[] args)
{
int a = 5;
doSomething( (double} a );
}
```

OVERLOADING METHODS

It can be useful to create multiple methods with the same method name, but with different parameter types. This can help the calling methods from having to *cast* the parameter to a required data type.

For example, we could create two versions of the *doSomething* method:

```
public static void doSomething (double d)
{//method contents }

public static void doSomething (int i)
{//method contents }
```

The calling method wouldn't need to specify which method to invoke. By sending a *double,* it would go to the first one, and by sending an *int* it would go to the second version.

```
public class MyClass {

public static void main(String[] args)
    {
    doSomething( 5 );  //a literal int
    doSomething(5.0);  //a literal double
    }
                                        Calls this method
    public static void doSomething (double d)
        {//method contents }
Calls this method
    public static void doSomething (int i)
        {//method contents }

} //end class MyClass
```

The programmer doesn't have to direct the message to the appropriate method. The compiler will determine the right destination based on parameter type, and will make the correct connection.

CHAPTER 5

ARRAYS

At this point you should have a pretty comfortable grasp of primitive variables – placeholders for primitive data. We have learned that before you can use a variable, it *must* be declared with the type of data it will contain. We also got practice doing the same thing with some non-primitive values – Strings.

```
int x; // declares a primitive variable x

int y = 5; //declares and initializes y

String s = "Foo"; //delares and initializes s
```

A problem with variables of this type is that we may have problems to solve that require a lot of variables, and declaring and assigning values to many variables can be tedious. For example, if I want to store the names of the days of the week in variables, I would need seven variables:

```
String day1 = "Sunday";
String day2 = "Monday";
String day3 = "Tuesday";
String day4 = "Wednesday";
String day5 = "Thursday";
String day6 = "Friday";
String day7 = "Saturday";
```

There **must** be a better way – alas there is! Let's learn about arrays…

WHAT IS AN ARRAY?

The easiest way to introduce Arrays is to describe them as containers. Think of them like a homogeneous bucket of data. They are homogeneous because you must declare what type of data they can contain, and you may not put any other type of data inside them.

Let's start with an example of one of the simplest data types we have used – the *int*. An *int* array can contain only primitive *int* values.

Recall that Java requires us to explicitly declare all variables with the type of data that they will eventually contain. By declaring a variable as an int, Java reserves enough memory to hold the largest integer that could possibly contain (±2,147,483,647.)

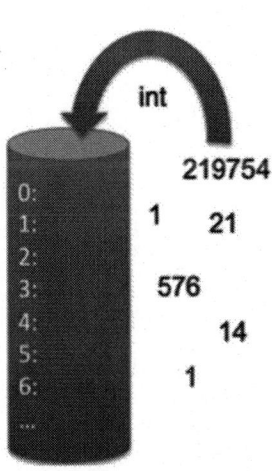

We must also declare the type of an array so Java can reserve sufficient memory for multiple *int* values. This means that we must also specify the size of the array when we create it. Arrays are always fixed in size – once we create them it's not possible to shrink or grown them.

There are two steps required to create an array, first we must declare a variable which will be the name of the array:

```
int[] myIntArray;
```

Declaring the array reserves that name for the array, but it doesn't actually create the container. As the second step, we must create the array and specify its size:

```
myIntArray = new int[10];
```

Note the use of the Java keyword *new* in the statement.

At this point, myIntArray is an array of size ten than can only contain primitive ints. When the array is created, all ten slots will contain 0's (zeros.)

Just as we can declare and initialize a variable all in one statement, we can also combine the two steps when initializing and creating an array:

```
int[] myIntArray = new int[10];
```

When we create an array, each position in the array is given an index number. Each index location is specified with an integer starting with 0 (zero.) We will use the index number to access that item in the array when it's needed (to retrieve the value contained at that location OR to change the value contained at that location.)

When we created the array named *myIntArray* above, the array has ten positions, each with a unique identifier based on its index number. Recall that when we create the *int* array, each position will contain the initial value 0 (zero.)

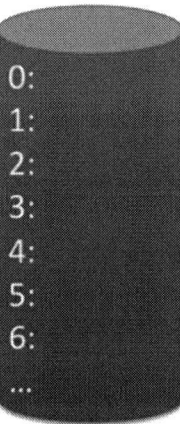

myIntArray[0]	0
myIntArray[1]	0
myIntArray[2]	0
myIntArray[3]	0
myIntArray[4]	0
myIntArray[5]	0
myIntArray[6]	0
myIntArray[7]	0
myIntArray[8]	0
myIntArray[9]	0

To change the value in one of the positions, we must assign the new value to the specific array location using the name we gave the array AND its index number:

```
myIntArray[2] = 12;
myIntArray[8] = 695;
```

The contents of those array locations will be changed, and the remaining array locations are unchanged:

myIntArray[0]	0
myIntArray[1]	0
myIntArray[2]	12
myIntArray[3]	0
myIntArray[4]	0
myIntArray[5]	0
myIntArray[6]	0
myIntArray[7]	0
myIntArray[8]	695
myIntArray[9]	0

RETRIEVING ARRAY CONTENTS

We can also retrieve the contents of one of the array positions using that same index location. If we want to retrieve the contents of our array at index location 8 and assign that value to the new variable y, we would write this expression:

```
int y = myIntArray[8];
```

For example, if we wanted to add the value 8 to the contents of the array at index location 2, then store the sum in new variable x, we would write the expression like this:

```
int x = myIntArray[2] + 8;
```

At this point, x will have the value 20.

POINT OF POSSIBLE CONFUSION

Now to a topic that often confuses students. Because the first index number is always zero, when we refer to the fifth element of the array, we are actually referring to the array at index location four. The first element of the array is at index location zero, the second element is at index location one, and so on. For an array of size ten, the largest index number will be nine.

In more abstract terms, an array of size n has index locations 0 through n-1.

LENGTH

It's not necessary to explicitly remember the size of an array you create. At any point in your program you can determine array's length using this syntax:

```
myIntArray.length;
```

Being mindful of the point of confusion just mentioned, bear in mind that the length of an array is the total number of positions that it contains. This is the same value that we specified when we originally created the array.

If we create an array like this:

```
int[] myIntArray = new int[10];
```

then if we write:

```
int a = myIntArray.length;
```

The variable a will contain the value 10.

However, if we were to then write the following expression...

```
myIntArray[a] = 50;
```

we would get a runtime error because there is not index location number 10 in an array of size 10. The largest index number in this array is 9. Note that this program WILL compile because the Java compiler will not evaluate the expression where the value of a is assigned to 10, so it can't know that this will exceed the maximum index number of the array. You won't discover the error until you actually run the program.

The error you will receive is: *IndexOutOfBoundsException*.

SAMPLE PROGRAM

Let's create a Java program that creates an array of ints and stores all the even numbers from 2 to 100 (inclusive.) This is a great example of the usefulness of an array. Without an array, we would need fifty variables to contain all those numbers!

Read each of the comments carefully for a description of what each statement is doing:

```
public class ArrayTest
{
public static void main(String[] args)
{
//declare an int array and create it with 50 positions
int[] myArray = new int[50];
//declare and initialize a variable to contain the first value in the array
int number = 2;
//loop using counter values 0 to 49. These will be used as array index locations
for(int i = 0; i < 50; i ++)
{
//set the contents of the array at index location i to the value in variable number
// the first time through the loop, index location 0 will be set to the value 2
//this loop will continue until index location 49 is set to the value 100
myArray[i] = number;
//increment the variable number by two. This will give only even numbers
number+= 2;
} //end for loop
```

```
//create another for loop from 0 to 49 and print out the array at each index location
//each number will be printed followed by a single space, all on the same line
for(int i = 0; i < 50; i++)
System.out.print(myArray[i] + " ");
//print a blank line
System.out.println();

}//end main

}// end class ArrayTest
```

The output of this program will be:

2 4 6 8 10 12 14 16 18 20 22 24 26 28 30 32 34 36 38 40 42 44 46 48 50 52 54 56 58 60 62 64 66 68 70 72 74 76 78 80 82 84 86 88 90 92 94 96 98 100

ARRAY INITIALIZERS

When creating a small array of primitive values, there's a shortcut that allows you declare the array variable, create the array, AND populate the array's values all in one statement:

```
int[] oddNumbers = {12, 3, 50, 7, 99};
```

The array index values are also automatically set, so kidsAges[1] contains 3, kidsAges[3] contains 7, etc. Also the value of kidsAges.length is 5.

USING A COUNTER TO SET THE ARRAY VALUE

If you need to create an array with a pattern of numbers, it's possible to use a loop to generate the number series and populate each element of the array. For example, to create an array with all the multiples of 11 up to 121, the following logic would create the array then populate it with the desired values.

```
public class TestArray
{
  public static void main(String[] args)
  {
  //Declare and create the array:
  int[] elevens = new int[11];

      //Create a loop that repeats 11 times
  //Start by setting the counter to 0 so you can
  //use the counter as the index value of the array

      for(int counter = 0; counter < 11; counter+=1)
      {
      //calculate the desired value based on the counter value
      //remember the counter starts at zero, so add one to it
      //before multiplying it by 11
```

```
        int value = (counter + 1) * 11; //11, 22, 33, etc.
        //put the calculated value in the array
        elevens[counter] = value;
        }//end for loop
    }//end main method
}//end class TestArray
```

You won't see anything when you run this program because there are no print statements. Add the following at the bottom of the main method to verify that the array contains the right values:

```
for(int c = 0; c <11; c++)
    System.out.print(elevens[c] + " ");
```

ENHANCED FOR STATEMENT

Looping through an array to populate its values or retrieve its values can be easily accomplished with either a *while* or a *for* loop as we just tried. There is also a special version of the *for* loop that can be used when you wish to retrieve every element of an array without the need for a counter. The approach eliminates any possibility of accidentally stepping outside the array (attempting to access an index location that is greater than the largest index location of the array.)

The syntax of the enhanced *for* statement is:

```
for (parameter : array-name)
    {
        java statements
    }
where:
        parameter has a variable name declared with its type
        array-name is the name of the array that you want to iterate
        through the parameter type MUST be the type that the array
        contains
```

This *for* statement may only be used for retrieving all the contents of an array. It cannot be used to modify the elements of an array.

Using the array we created in the previous section, recall that we included the following "counter controlled repetition" code to retrieve and print the contents of the array we created:

```
for(int c = 0; c <11; c++)
    System.out.print(elevens[c] + " ");
```

Using the enhanced *for* statement, we would rewrite this loop like this:

```
for(int arrayValue : elevens)
    System.out.print(arrayValue + " ");
```

Note that in the first version, the loop counter(c) is used as the index value in the array when retrieving its contents. In the second version, there is no counter variable. The variable we named *arrayValue* is used to store the contents of one slot in the array, prints that value, then replaces the contents of *arrayValue* with the next element of the array, and so on. This repeats until the last element of the array has been rerieved.

PASSING ARRAYS TO METHODS

REMINDER: When we learned how to pass parameters from one method to another, remember that we didn't actually pass the variable, we passed *the contents of that variable*. In the example below, when we pass *x* to *otherMethod*, we are actually passing the contents of x (which is the integer value 5.) When *otherMethod* starts, the first thing it does is declare variable *y* and set its value to the integer that was passed to it.

```
public static void main(String[] args)
{
int x = 5;
otherMethod(x);
}

public static void otherMethod(int y)
{
System.out.println(y);
}
```

If we wish to pass an array from one method to another, the code would look like this:

```
public static void main(String[] args)
{
int[] x = {1,3,5,7,9};
otherMethod(x);
}

public static void otherMethod(int[] y)
{

}
```

Note that when we pass variable *x* from the main method, we are passing the *contents of x*, which is the entire array. When *otherMethod* begins, the first thing it does is declare variable *y* as an int array. In *otherMethod*, the contents of *y* is the array we created in the main method.

If we change the contents of the array named *y* in the method *otherMethod*, those changes will be reflected when we return to the main method.

To demonstrate this, let's add a line of code in *otherMethod*, that doubles the values of each element of the array:

```
public static void otherMethod(int[] y)
{
//double the value of each element of array y

for(int c = 0; c < y.length; c++)
y[c] = y[c] * 2; //we could have also used y[c] *= 2

}
```

Now let's add a statement at the bottom of the *main* method that prints the contents of array x when control is returned to *main* after *otherMethod* is finished:

```
public static void main(String[] args)
{
int[] x = {1,3,5,7,9};
otherMethod(x);
//print the contents of array x using the enhanced for statement
for(int arrayElement : x)
  System.out.print(arrayElement + " ");
}
```

The following will print when the program is run:

```
2  6  10  14  18
```

This may seem confusing at first, because if you just evaluate the code in the main method, it appears that the contents of array *x* was never changed. However, there is only one array. It goes by the name *x* when in the main method, and it goes by the name *y* when in *otherMethod*.

So for practice, evaluate the code and determine what will print when the following program is run:

```
public class MyClass
{
    public static void main(String[] args)          myArray
    {
    int[] myArray = {1, 2, 3, 4, 5};
    otherMethod(myArray);
    System.out.println(myArray[1]);
    }

    public static void otherMethod(int[] passedArray)
    {
    passedArray[1] = 99;
    System.out.println(passedArray[1]);
    }
}
```

Again, since there is only one array that goes by different names in each of the methods, changes that occur in *otherMethod* will be reflected in *main*. The output of this program will be:

```
99
99
```

ARRAYS WITH OTHER TYPES

So far, all our examples have been with arrays contain ints. An array can actually contain any type of element. Just remember that arrays are *homogeneous* – all elements must be of the type that the array is declared to contain.

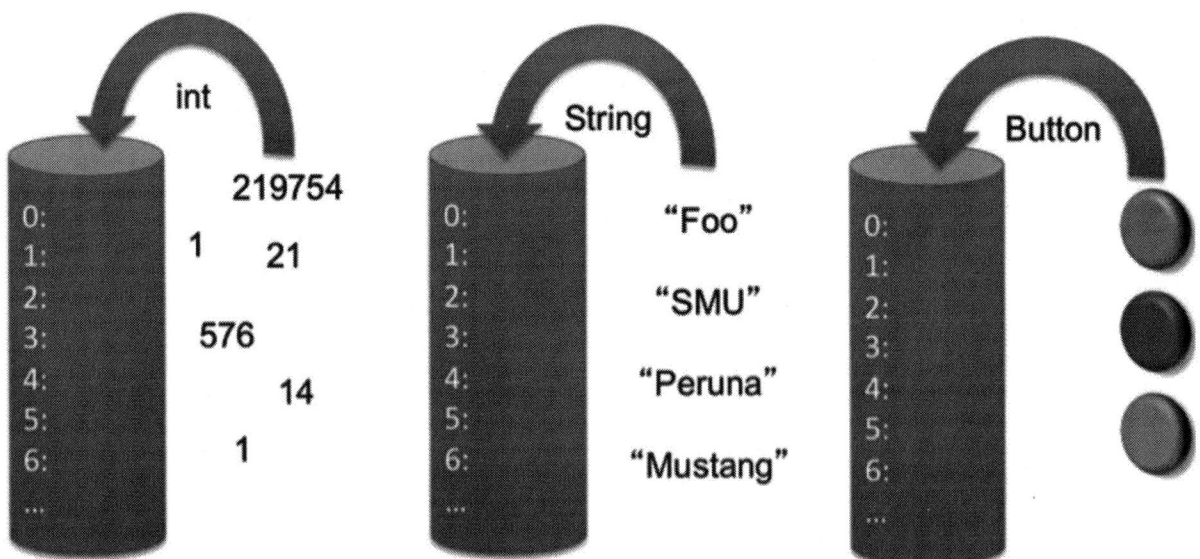

We use the same syntax we used for int arrays to declare and create arrays of other types. Just be sure to declare the correct type. For example, let's look at the day of week problem presented at the beginning of this chapter. We would start by creating a String array of size 7:

```
String[] dayNames = new String[7];
```

Since Strings can't be easily derived from a formula, we would likely populate the String array with a series of statements as follows:

```
dayNames[0] = "Sunday";
dayNames[1] = "Monday";
dayNames[2] = "Tuesday";
dayNames[3] = "Wednesday";
dayNames[4] = "Thursday";
dayNames[5] = "Friday";
dayNames[6] = "Saturday";
```

That may not seem any more convenient than creating seven unique variables like we showed at the beginning of the chapter. However, look how easy it is to retrieve all the day names once the array is populated:

```
for(int c = 0; c < 7; c++)
    System.out.print(dayNames[c] + " ");
```

The resulting output would be:

```
Sunday Monday Tuesday Wednesday Thursday Friday Saturday
```

In this example, since we're retrieving all the contents of the array, we could also use the enhanced *for* statement:

```
for(String s : dayNames)
    System.out.print(s + " ");
```

Notice that each element that is retrieved from the array is a String, so we declare variable *s* as a String to store each element of the String array as they are retrieved.

So we have seen that Arrays can ints and they can also contain Strings. They can also contain any of the other seven primitive types. Additionally, arrays can contain any type of *object*. We'll learn how to do this when we learn object oriented programming later.

MULTI-DIMENSIONAL ARRAYS

A helpful way to understand arrays is to think of an array as a single column in a spreadsheet:

	A
1	2
2	4
3	5
4	6
5	9
6	88

Just be careful with this representation because spreadsheet row numbers usually begin with 1, and array index numbers begin with 0 (zero.)

Now think of a spreadsheet with two columns:

	A	B
1	2	10
2	4	20
3	5	30
4	6	40
5	9	50
6	88	60

How would we handle this with Java? This is where multi-dimensional arrays are used. Multidimensional arrays require two index numbers to set or retrieve each element. To more easily map to the spreadsheet example, let's replace the spreadsheet row numbers and column letters with index numbers so we can treat it as though it was a Java array:

	0	1
0	2	10
1	4	20
2	5	30
3	6	40
4	9	50
5	88	60

In the previous illustration, the number 50 can be found at row 5, column B. In the second illustration, the number 50 is found at row 4, column 1. The structure is the same, you just have to get comfortable with refer-ring to an element of the array by using two index values. In Java we always specify the row number first.

To create a two-dimensional array in Java, use the following syntax:

```
int[][] arrayName = new int[totalRows][totalColumns];
```

So, we would create the array depicted in the spreadsheet example above as follows:

```
int[][] myValues = new int[6][2];
```

We use 6 and 2 because there are six rows (index numbers 0 to 5) and two columns (index numbers 0 to 1). At this point, the array has been created. Since we haven't set any values yet, all the elements of the array will be 0 (zero) because primitive arrays always populate with a default value.

	0	1
0	0	0
1	0	0
2	0	0
3	0	0
4	0	0
5	0	0

If we wanted to populate one element in this two-dimensional array, we must use both index numbers. To set the value of row 0, column 0 we write:

```
myValues[0][0] = 2;
```

Let's set a few more values:

```
myValues[0][1] = 4;
myValues[0][2] = 5;
myValues[0][3] = 6;
myValues[0][4] = 9;
myValues[0][5] = 99;
```

Our array now looks like this:

	0	1
0	2	0
1	4	0
2	5	0
3	6	0
4	9	0
5	88	0

Since we want the second column to contain a pattern of numbers, populating its values is easier – we can use a loop. We'll use a counter to represent the row index numbers, and we'll use the fixed value 1 for the column number:

```
int value = 10;
for(int c = 0; c <= 5; c++)
{
  myValues[c][1] = value;
  value += 10;
}
```

Now our array looks like this:

	0	1
0	2	10
1	4	20
2	5	30
3	6	40
4	9	50
5	88	60

When creating an array that doesn't contain primitive values, the default value of each element is empty, or "nothing." In Java we refer to this with the keyword *null*. This is true for any array of non-primitives whether it's one-dimensional or multi-dimensional.

Let's create a two-dimensional array of Strings using the same format shown for the int array:

```
String[][] myStringArray = new String[4][3];
```

The resulting array looks like this:

	0	1	2	3
0	null	null	null	null
1	null	null	null	null
2	null	null	null	null
3	null	null	null	null

If we want to put the value "Foo" at the first row and second column, we would write the following statement:

```
myStringArray[0][1] = "Foo";
```

The resulting array:

	0	1	2	3
0	null	Foo	null	null
1	null	null	null	null
2	null	null	null	null
3	null	null	null	null

Java doesn't have a nice utility to display the contents of an array. Instead, we must write a loop with print statements. The following program will loop through the String array we just created. Note that since we have to navigate both rows and columns, we will need to use a nested *for* loop – a loop inside a loop:

```
public class Practice
{
public static void main(String[] args)
{
String[][] myArray = new String[4][3];
myArray[0][1] = "Foo";
for(int i = 0; i < 4; i++)
{
   for(int j = 0; j< 3; j++)
     System.out.printf("\nLocation %d , %d contains: %s", i , j, myArray[i][j]);
}//end "outer" for loop
}//end main method
}//end class Practice
```

Just like with one-dimensional arrays, there is a shortcut to create a two-dimensional array with its contents:

```
int[][] myArray = { {1,2},{3,4}};
```

When we use this shortcut approach, it's not necessary to specify the size of the array. Java will determine this automatically based on the number of elements you specify. The array myArray will have two rows and two columns. The outer curly braces contain the contents of each row, and the inner curly braces contain the contents of each column with each row. To demonstrate this, we can write an embedded loop:

```
public class TestArray2
{
public static void main(String[] args)
{
  //declare and create the contents of a two-dimensional array
  int[][] myArray = {{1,2},{3,4}};

  for(int a = 0; a < 2; a++) //instead of 2 we could have used myArray.length
    {
    for(int b = 0; b < 2; b++) //instead of 2 we could have used myArray.length
      {
      System.out.printf("row %d column %d contains %d \n",a,b,myArray[a][b]);
      }//end inner for loop
    }//end outer for loop
  }//end main
}//end class
```

It's not necessary for all each row in a multi-dimensional array to have the same number of columns. For example, the following will create an array with two elements in the first row, one element in the second row, and three elements in the third row:

```
int[][] myArray = { { 1, 2 } , { 3 } , { 4, 5, 6 } } ;
```

To create this array without the shortcut, the size of the column is not specified when initially creating the array:

```
int[][] myArray = new int[3][];
```

The size of each row must then be specified in separate statements:

```
myArray[0] = new int[2];
myArray[1] = new int[1];
myArray[2] = new int[3];
```

Just be careful when navigating arrays like this with a loop because it's easy to accidentally go outside the boundaries of one of the rows.

⟍ PASSING DATA INTO YOUR JAVA PROGRAM

Up to this point, you have written many programs that contain an array that you've been ignoring. Look for the square brackets in the following Java code:

```
public static void main(String[] args)
```

Notice that the parameter of the *main* method named *args* is declared as an array of Strings.

When you run one of your Java programs, you can include additional information to pass into your program. If additional information is included, the Java Virtual Machine will create the *args* String array and populate it with your data.

For example, the following Java program prints out the contents of the first element of the *args* array:

```java
public class Practice
{
  public static void main(String[] args)
  {
  System.out.println(args[0]);
  }
}
```

Although you can successfully compile this program, when you run it you'll get a runtime error because the *args* array hasn't been created. Therefore there is nothing at args[0].

Instead, try running the program and pass in data:

```
C:\>java MyClass Foo
```

The output will be:

```
Foo
```

You can pass in as many values as you want when launching your program. A blank space specifies separation between each element. If we run the same program above as follows:

```
C:\>java MyClass Red Green Blue Yellow
```

The *args* array will be size 4 with the following contents:

args[0]	Red
args[1]	Green
args[2]	Blue
args[3]	Yellow

Since a space is the separator between the elements, if you want to include a space as part of one of one of the elements you must surround it with double quotes. The following will create the *args* array as size 2:

args[0]	Red Apple
args[1]	Green Pepper

```
C:\>java MyClass "Red Apple" "Green Pepper"
```

Be careful when passing numbers into the *args* array. All elements are treated as Strings. Therefore the numbers 1, 12.5 and 5000 will be treated as "1," "12.5" and "5000."

```
C:\>java MyClass 1 12.5 5000
```

args[0]	1
args[1]	12.5
args[2]	5000

To bring these values into your program as numbers, you must convert them from String to integers or doubles using the following static methods in library classes Integer and Double:

```
int x = Integer.parseInt("5000"); // creates integer x with value 5000

double d = Double.parseDouble("12.5"); // creates double d with value 12.5
```

Repeating the previous example, when we run the following:

```
C:\>java MyClass 1 12.5 5000
```

Simply convert the values of args[0], args[1] and args[2] in your program:

```
int x = Integer.parseInt(args[0]);
double d = Double.parseDouble(args[1]);
int y = Integer.parseInt(args[2]);
```

Of course this isn't foolproof – you must know what type of data will be passed in, and it must be passed in the correct order.

Finally, if you don't know how many elements will be passed in when writing your program, you can create a loop to iterate through the args array. Just use *args.length* as the upper limit when writing the loop. In this example, the *for loop* will be bypassed if the args array is empty, otherwise it will continue to loop until it reaches the size of the *args* array:

```
public class Practice
{
  public static void main(String[] args)
  {
  for(int i = 0; i < args.length; i++)
    System.out.println(args[i]);
  }
}
```

ARRAYS LIBRARY CLASS

The library class *Arrays* provides several utilitarian static methods that can be used to perform common array manipulations. It must be imported to use:

```
import java.util.Arrays;
```

Arrays.sort

The sort method will sort an array containing primitives: int, double, float, short, long, char, or byte elements. It can also sort non-primitive objects such as Strings.

The following program creates two arrays, sorts them, and prints the sorted array contents:

```
import java.util.Arrays;
public class Practice
{
  public static void main(String[] args)
  {
  String[] a = {"B", "A", "C", "D"};
  int[] b = { 5, 4, 3, 2};
```

```
Arrays.sort(b);
Arrays.sort(a);

for(String aString : a)
  System.out.printf("%s ",aString);

for(int anInt : b )
  System.out.prinft("%d ",anInt);

}//end main
}//end class Practice
```

The output will be:

```
A B C D 2 3 4 5
```

Arrays.binarySearch

This method requires two parameters – the array you would like to search, and the value you would like to search for. It returns the index value of the element it finds.

A couple things to note:

- Binary search only works with a sorted array, so you MUST sort the array before using this method.
- If the array contains more than one of the values you're searching for, it just returns the index of the first one it finds.
- If the value isn't found in the array, this method returns the size of the array as a negative number.

```
import java.util.Arrays;
public class Practice
{
    public static void main(String[] args)
    {
    int x;
    int[] myArray = {1, 3, 5, 2, 6, 5, 5, 77, 2, 5};

    Arrays.sort(myArray); //Must sort before using binary search

    x =Arrays.binarySearch(myArray,77);
    System.out.println("Found 77 at index location " + x);


    //IF MORE THAN ONE FOUND, UNRELIABLE WHICH IS RETURNED
    //BECAUSE BINARY SEARCH DOES NOT SEARCH FRONT TO BACK
    x =Arrays.binarySearch(myArray,5);
    System.out.println("Found 5 at index location " + x);

    //IF NOT FOUND, Returns -(arraySize++)
    x =Arrays.binarySearch(myArray,9);
    System.out.println("Found 9 at index location " + x);

    }//end main method
}//end class Practice
```

Output from running the program:

```
Found 77 at index location 9
Found 5 at index location 4
Found 9 at index location -10
```

A good strategy with the binarySearch method is to use an if..else statement which returns "not found" if a negative number is returned. For example:

```
int y = 9;
int x = Arrays.binarySearch(myArray,y);
if(x >= 0)
   System.out.println("Found " + y + " at index location " + x);
else
   System.out.println("Not found.");
```

Arrays.fill

The fill method is quick way to fill up an array giving all elements the same value. The value must match the type of the array.

```
import java.util.Arrays;
public class Practice
{
    public static void main(String[] args)
    {
    int[] myArray = {1, 3, 5, 7};
    Arrays.fill(myArray,9);
    for(int i = 0; i < myArray.length; i++)
      System.out.print(myArray[i] + " ");
    }
}
```

Although this array was created with values 1, 3, 5 and 7, those values will all be replaced with the integer 9. The output from running this program is:

```
9 9 9 9
```

System.arraycopy

Sometimes it's helpful to make a copy of an array. You must be careful when using multiple variables to reference an array because you may thinking you're creating a copy when you are actually just creating multiple names to reference the same array.

Evaluate the following code and determine what will be printed:

```
int[] b = { 5, 4, 3, 2};

int[] c = b;

c[0] = 99;

for(int x : b) //PRINT THE CONTENTS OF ARRAY b
   System.out.print(x + " ");
```

```
System.out.println();

for(int x : c) //PRINT THE CONTENTS OF ARRAY c
  System.out.print(x + " ");
```

In the second line, we are not assigning a copy of array b to variable c, we are just creating a second name to refer to the same array. Therefore, the output from running this program is:

```
99  4  3  2
99  4  3  2
```

If you want to create a brand new array which contains a copy of all the elements of another array, use *System. arraycopy*. The format of *arraycopy* is:

```
System.arraycopy(array1, startIndex, array2, destIndex, numElements)
```

This copies *numElements* elements from *array1* starting at index location *startIndex* into *array2* starting at *destIndex*.

You have to be very careful with *arraycopy* to ensure that both arrays have already been declared and created, and the contents from the first array will fit into the second array. See the example below:

```
public class Practice
{
        public static void main(String[] args)
        {
        int[] myArray = {1, 3, 5, 7};
        int[] newArray = new int[4];
        int[] otherArray = new int[2];
        int[] yetAnotherArray;

        System.arraycopy(myArray,0,newArray,0,4);
        for(int i = 0; i < newArray.length; i++)
          System.out.println(newArray[i]);

        //THIS WILL THROW IndexOutOfBoundsException
        System.arraycopy(myArray,0,otherArray,0,4);

        //THIS WON'T COMPILE BECAUSE yetAnotherArray IS NULL
        //System.arraycopy(myArray,0,yetAnotherArray,0,4);
        }
}
```

CHAPTER 6

OBJECT ORIENTED PROGRAMMING

At this point we are going to make a significant shift in the way we construct computer programs. Recall that when we started, we developed algorithms that were fully contained in one method (main) in one class. We then learned how to break some of the functionality out of the *main* method and put it in other methods. This helped us avoid creating a very large *main* method that would be hard to maintain. Next, we'll learn how to break functionality out into multiple classes, which will lead us into object-oriented programming.

INTERCHANGEABLE PARTS

Most people who grew up in the United States remember learning about Eli Whitney and his famed cotton gin. Not only did his invention revolutionize farming, but it also revolutionized the way machines were built. Whitney's used a relatively unknown practice of creating a machine from interchangeable parts when designing the cotton gin. His motivation was to reduce the maintenance burden on the device. When a part breaks, replacing or repairing that part was a straightforward process that gets the machine back in working order much faster and less costly than repairing or replacing an entire machine would have been.

© Underwood & Underwood/Corbis

Ironically, the innovation of interchangeable parts because Whitney's undoing. Because the machine was easily constructor, imitators ran amuck. Whitney scrambled to file a patent in 1794, but that slow process didn't offer an enforceable patent until 15 years later. Whitney had spent his life's earnings fighting patent infringement.

Whitney didn't give up, though. During this same period he used the same engineering strategy to redesign muskets. He actually testified before the U.S. Congress while demonstrating how easy it was to repair one of these modular muskets without having to send it from the battlefield back for a gunsmith to work on. This invention did bring wealth to Whitney because his new easily repairable muskets became a prominent part of the War of 1812.

BUILDING FROM COMPONENTS

Most of the things we use in our life are made from parts. Just look around where you are right now—pick anything. It's most likely made up of parts. A couch has legs, arms, cushions, nails, staples, etc. Each one of these parts has individual value by itself, but its value increases tremendously by contributing to the "bigger thing—the couch.

© Dimedrol68, 2013. Used under license from Shutterstock, Inc.

Let's use a bike as another example. It's possible to build a bike from scratch using raw materials such as aluminum, steel, rubber, wire, etc. With the proper tools (and a lot of patience!) you could cut, bend, and mold the material into a working bicycle.

Not only is that a lot of trouble, but it's also fraught with potential problems. There are countless possible quality issues with a bike built this way.

Instead, we typically build a bike from parts. Each part is an independently important thing by itself, but which contributes to the overall value and utility of the bike. A few of the bike parts are:

- Seat
- Frame
- Fork
- Brake
- Pedal
- Chain
- Cables
- Tires
- Tubes
- Nuts
- Seat post
- Handlebar
- Gear Shifter
- Brake Lever
- Sprocket
- Derailleur
- Wheels
- Spokes
- Bolts
- …

The list could go on and on. And actually, many of the parts listed are actually made up of multiple smaller parts. For example, consider the derailleur, which is the device attached to the back wheel that moves the chain from sprocket to sprocket. Although we refer to it as one part, we could actually break open its housing and see many parts contained inside it.

A bike manufacturer probably doesn't even make its own derailleurs or brakes. There are companies that specialize in just making these parts to sell to multiple bike manufacturers. The derailleur manufacturer focuses on the quality of their component, giving the bike manufacturer the ability to attach it to the bike and know that it will perform its limited set of critical functions well.

SHIFTING TO OBJECTS

Up to this point we have been doing *procedural* programming. Our programs have been linear, with a definitive start and end. It's possible to put any of the programs we've built into a single *main* method in a single class, although we learned how to break up the main method into multiple smaller methods for the purpose of organization and managing complexity. This linear approach works well when developing solutions to small problems. However, for large complex systems, this approach doesn't work well.

As an example, consider an insurance company's claims system. When you experience a loss and call your insurance company to report a claim, the person you are talking to is most likely using a computer program to record the details of the loss. With the

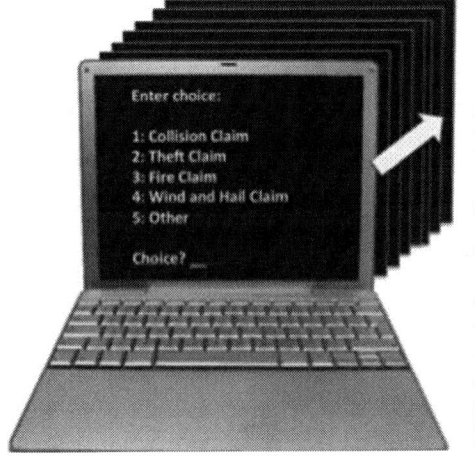

procedural programming approach, the system would be linear with a definitive starting and ending point.

The insurance claims rep would need to maintain complete control of the phone conversation because the system prescribes the sequence of questions that are asked. Traditional programs written in this manner were referred to as "green screen" programs because they were all text based systems that often had white text on a green background.

Imagine a customer calling in to report the collision they had with a tree. The claims rep may start asking questions about the weather at the time of the accident while the customer is urgently wanting to talk about his injuries. The claims rep must tell the customer to wait, because that screen is several pages away in the sequence. This can be very frustrating for the customer and for the claims rep.

Instead, imagine a claims system that looks more like your Windows or Mac computer—with folders and icons that can be dragged, moved, opened, copied, etc. With this "object oriented" user interface, the claims rep could pull "forms" for various parts of the interview as they fit the conversation. The system could still keep track of what's missing to advise the claims rep prior to ending the call. However, this flexibility is much more natural and is likely a better experience for the customer.

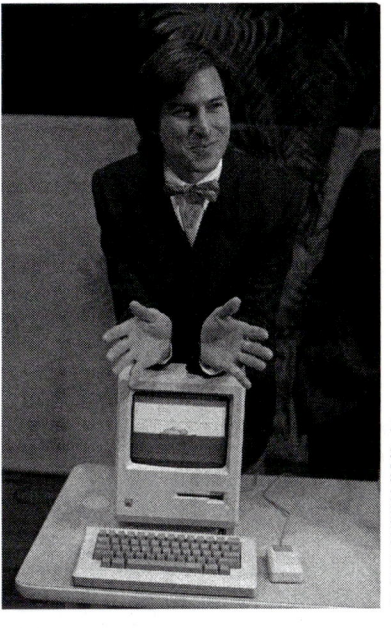

The object oriented user interface, which we often refer to as "GUI" or Graphical User Interface, was developed by Alan Kay, Adele Goldberg and their team at Xerox's PARC lab in California in the early 1970s. The first GUI was built using a language named Smalltalk.

Xerox chose not to pursue commercialization of the technology, and instead, accepted an invitation to demonstrate it to Steve Jobs, co-founder of Apple. Jobs used the ideas he learned to create the Apple's Lisa computer, the predecessor to their legendary Macintosh, now simply referred to as the Mac.

BASIC OBJECT ORIENTED PROGRAMMING CONCEPTS

Let's introduce object oriented programming with a metaphor—a cheesecake pan. When you mix the ingredients, pour them into the pan and bake it, you get a cheesecake.

You can repeat the process and create multiple cheesecakes using the same pan. They may all look identical, but you know that each cake is unique.

To put this in object oriented terms, the mold is the *class* and the resulting cakes are instances. Each cake conforms to the parameters of the mold, although each might look slightly different. You might even choose to vary the ingredients in some instances.

CLASS

In object oriented programming, when we construct a class, we are creating a blueprint from which objects can be "stamped out." This is just like when a car manufacturer creates cars from a standard design. Each car *instance* from one blueprint has the same dimensions, features, and capabilities. There could be some variation among the instances. For example, each car may be painted a different color.

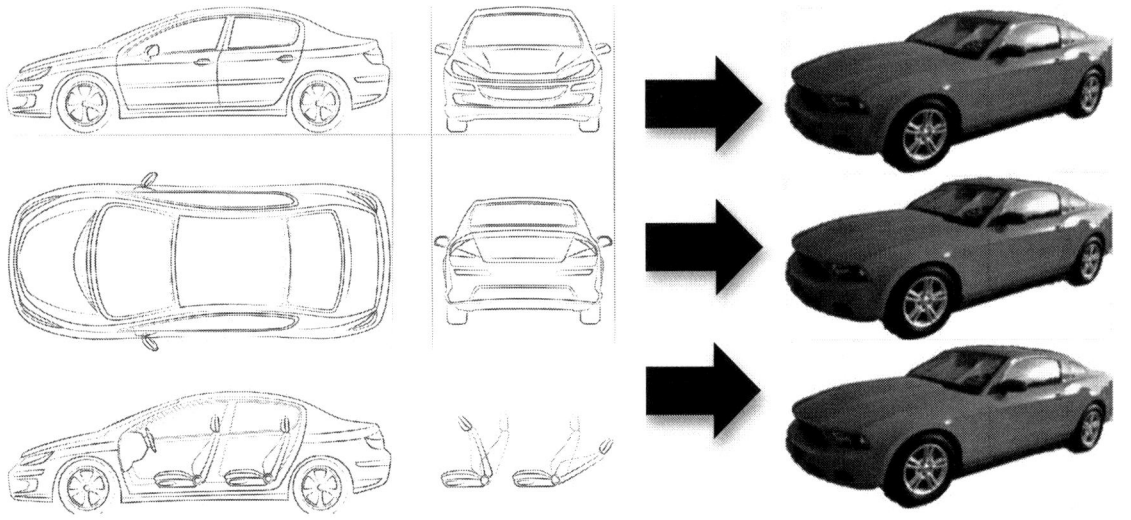

The class will specify a list of placeholders for information we want to remember about each instance. These are called *attributes*, or *instance variables*. The car class would include variables that are declared with a type, but with no values assigned to them.

For the car example, possible attributes are year, make, model, color, vehicle identification number, etc. In Java, the class we've described so far looks like this:

```
public class Car
{
  int year;
  String make;
  String model;
  String color;
}
```

Note that we are not assigning values to Car's four variables. We'll do that later when we create intances, or Car objects.

One additional step is recommended when declaring variables in a class. We want to ensure that each car's data is protected from being viewed or changed without a Car's knowledge. This is called *encapsulation*.

A different example that motivates the importance of this is you and your name. Let's say we have a class called "Person" with attributes name and socialSecurityNumber. Next, let's say you are an instance of person with values for both of these attributes. If another person asked you what your social security number is, you would want to decide whether or not to tell them. If you choose, you could reject or ignore the request.

Without *encapsulation*, the other person could reach in and grab the value of your social security number without your permission. We implement encapsulation (or "information hiding") in Java with what's referred to as an *access modifier* called *private*. By putting the keyword *private* in front of each variable declaration, we are preventing other objects from "messing with" our attribute values – they can't be changed and can't be retrieved.

```
public class Car
{
  private int year;
  private String make;
  private String model;
  private String color;
}
```

So if these attribute values can't be viewed or changed, how can they be used? They are viewed and changed only through methods defined within the class. By using the access modifier *public* in front of a method declaration, other objects can ask an object to invoke one of its public methods. We can include logic inside one of these methods that changes or retrieves the value of a private attribute.

Let's add two public methods to our class Car – one to change the value of the private attribute *color* and one to retrieve the value of color:

```
public class Car
{
  private int year;
  private String make;
  private String model;
  private String color;

  public void setColor(String s)
  {
    color = s;
  }

  public String getColor()
  {
    return color;
  }
}
```

In this example, if another object wishes to get the color of the car, it can invoke the Car object's public *getColor* method, which will return the contents of the private attribute *color*.

Think of a class as a donut, with the private attributes (data) in the middle, and the public methods on the perimeter.

Other objects can interact with an object by executing its public methods. We call this "sending a message" to an object.

Next we'll create some Car objects/instances so we can demonstrate this interaction.

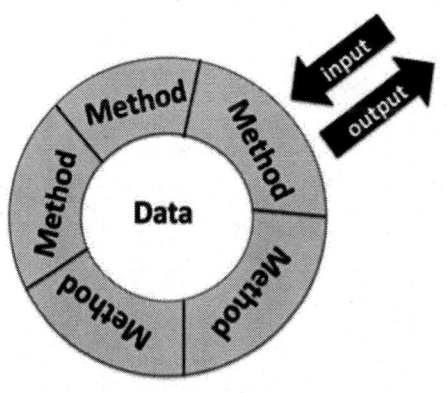

OBJECT

To create an instance of a class, we must use the keyword *new*. Recall using *new* when using Scanner and Random? We were actually creating instances of the class Scanner and Random. The basic structure of the statement we use to create an instance of a class is:

```
ClassName variableName = new ClassName();
```

See how Scanner and Random fit this structure:

```
Scanner input = new Scanner(System.in);
Random r = new Random();
```

So for our Car class, we would create a Car instance or object like this:

```
Car myCar = new Car();
```

On the right side of the expression, a new instance of the Car class is created. On the left side, we declare a variable (myCar) of type Car. In other words, we are creating the name *myCar* to refer to one instance of the class Car.

So where do we create these objects? We don't create a Car object within the Car class. We use a method in another class to create these objects. For now, we can create a *main* method in a test class to create and test these objects.

If we wanted to create multiple Car instances, each one would require its own variable and its own new statement:

```
public class Tester {
    public static void main(String[] args)
    {
    Car myCar = new Car();
    Car myOtherCar = new Car();
    Car yetAnotherCar = new Car();
    }//end main
}//end class
```

As each car is created, it occupies a unique location in the computer's RAM. We then use the variable names we created to communicate with each instance.

To communicate with one of those car instances (object) we simply "send it a message," which means we invoke one of its methods.

The syntax for sending a message is to put a period at the end of the variable name we are using to reference the object, followed by the name of one of its methods. Be sure to include the parentheses, which may or may not have parameters within it, and terminate the statement with a semicolon.

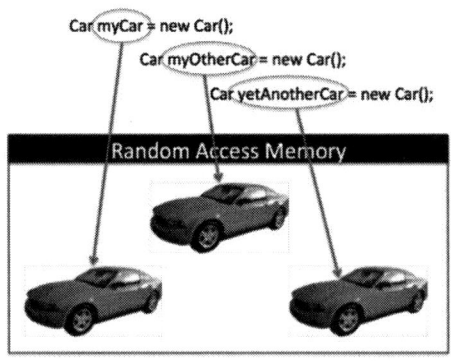

Syntax for sending a message:

```
objectName.methodName(parameters);
```

So we can send a message to one of our Car objects to change the value of its color to red as follows:

```
myCar.setColor("red");
```

When sending a message to a Car object, we must specify which Car instance we are talking to by using the variable name we declared when we created it. In the illustration below, the instances *myCar* and *myOtherCar* each manage their own private data. We change the value of the *color* attribute by sending the public message *setColor* to each object separately.

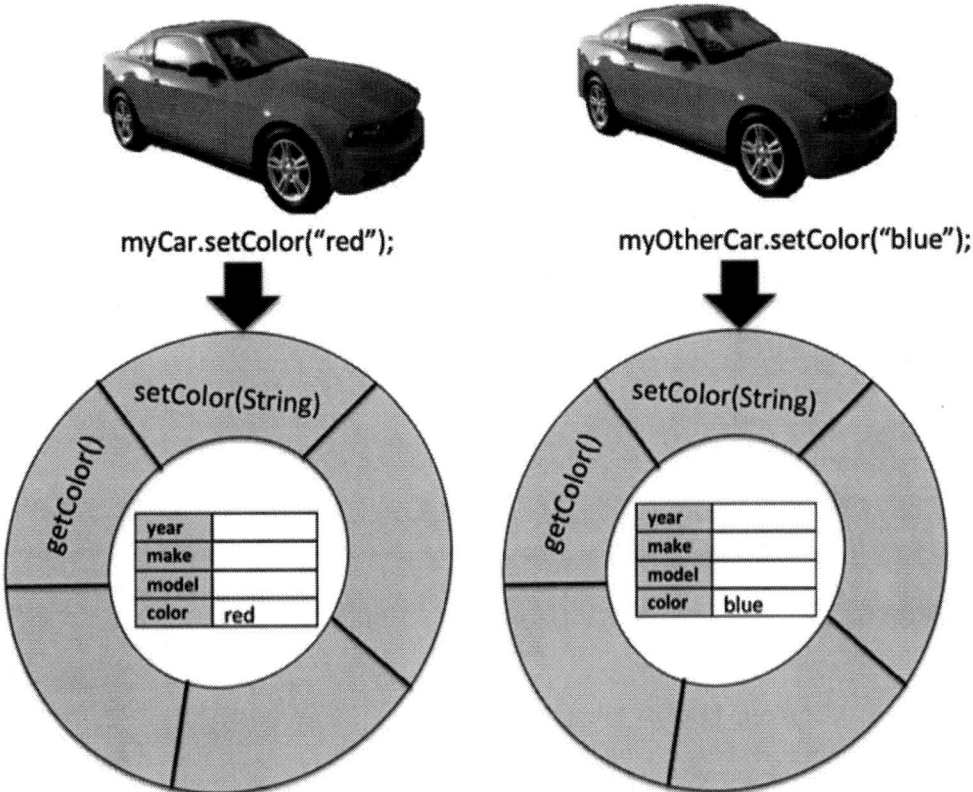

Sending a public message (invoking a public method) to an object is the only way we can change the value of one of its private attributes. If we tried the following, our program wouldn't compile because we are not permitted to directly access a private variable from anywhere except a method within the class we're in.

```
myCar.color = "red"; //Won't work!
```

In this example, from within the *main* method in our Tester class, we have access to the three Car variables we declared (and the objects they reference.) Through those objects, we are also able to invoke any public method in the Car class. We cannot, however, access any of the private attributes in the Car class.

STATIC VS. NON-STATIC

Prior to introducing object oriented programming, we included the keyword "static" in the signature of the methods we wrote. Static means that the method belongs to the class itself, and it can be invoked directly on the class like this:

```
ClassName.staticMethodName();
```

Static methods are commonly used to implement function libraries, such as those found in the library class *Math*. For example, to call a function that returns the maximum value of two numbers, we invoke the *max* method directly on the class itself:

```
Math.max(5,10);
```

The use of *static* methods is not often used in modern programming, but can be useful in situations where simple utilitarian functions are needed and objects are not warranted.

By excluding the *static* keyword in a method signature, a method is by default *non-static*, meaning the method becomes a "behavior" of all of the instances of that class.

The one static method that we will continue to use is the *main* method. When you pass a compiled Java program to the Java Virtual Machine, the JVM looks for the static *main* method. So if we entered *java Tester* on the command line, the JVM is essentially invoking *Tester.main()*.

While there may be appropriate uses of *static* methods, and there are uses of *static* variables as well, we will avoid them (other than the *main* method) as we solidify our object-oriented programming experience.

CONSTRUCTORS

There is a special type of method we create in our classes that is used when creating instances. These are called *constructors*. They look similar to other methods, but have two distinct differences:

1. The constructor name is the same as the class name.
2. The constructor has **no** return type (e.g., String, void, int)

A constructor doesn't need to declare a return type because its return type is implicit – it always returns and instance of the class it is contained in.

You have actually been using constructors frequently in most of the programs you have written up to this point.

Recall that we created a Car instance like this:

```
Car myCar = new Car();
```

The method following the *new* keyword on the right side is a constructor. If we don't create a constructor in our class, a default (invisible) constructor is created for us. In the case of *Car*, we didn't create a constructor, but the constructor *Car()* is still available for us to use.

When *new Car()* is invoked, the default constructor will create the instance and assign default values to its instance variables. The default values are zero for all numeric primitive instance variables, *false* for boolean instance variables, and *null* for everything else.

To create our own constructor for *Car*, we use the structure shown below and include any logic we wish to execute when each *Car* instance is created:

```
public class Car
{
  private int year;
  private String make;
  private String model;
  private String color;
```

```
public Car()
{
  year = 1900;
  make = "Unknown";
  model = "Unknown";
  color = "Unknown";
}

  public void setColor(String s)
  {
    color = s;
  }

  public String getColor()
  {
    return color;
  }
}
```

So now when we invoke *new Car()*, instead of the default constructor the constructor we built will be executed. This is useful for setting default values to each instance variable when creating new instances of a class.

We can also create multiple versions of a constructor. Since the constructor name is also the name of the class, when we create multiple constructors, the only way we can make them unique is by giving each different parameters. Multiple versions of a constructor is called *overloading* a constructor. We introduced the concept of *overloading* with methods.

As an example example, here are four examples of creating *Car* instances with four different versions of the *Car* constructor:

```
Car c1 = new Car();
Car c2 = new Car(2013);
Car c3 = new Car(2013,"Ford","Mustang");
Car c4 = new Car(2013,"Ford","Mustang", "red");
```

The four constructors that we need to put inside our *Car* class are:

```
public Car() {
   year = 1900;
   make = "Unknown";
   model = "Unknown";
   color = "Unknown";
}

public Car(int x) {
   year = x;
   make = "Unknown";
   model = "Unknown";
   color = "Unknown";
}
```

```
public Car(int x, String a, String b) {
    year = x;
    make = a;
    model = b;
    color = "Unknown";
}

public Car(int x, String a, String b, String c) {
    year = x;
    make = a;
    model = b;
    color = c;
}
```

Our class is starting to take shape now. It has attributes, constructors, and methods for getting or setting values of the color attribute. For completeness, let's create getter and setter methods for the other three attributes. It's a good programming practice to create a public getter and setter method for each of the attributes in a class.

The format of a getter method always has a simple return statement that returns the contents of the variable it represents. There are no parameters in a getter method. The getter method signature must have a return type that matches the type of the variable whose contents are being returned.

```
public variableType getVariableName()
{
 return variableName;
}
```

So using this format, the getters for year (an int) and make and model (both Strings) would look like this:

```
public int getYear ()
{
 return year;
}

public String getMake ()
{
 return make;
}

public String getModel ()
{
 return model;
}
```

The setter method always has no return statement, so the return type is always void. The setter also has a single parameter which is used to pass in a value to assign to the variable it represents. Inside the setter method, simply put an assignment statement. The value that's passed into the method (which is in a temporary variable that's declared in parameter part of the method signature) will be assigned to the instance variable.

```
public void setVariableName(variableType tempVariableName)
{

  variableName = tempVariableName;

}
```

So using this format, the setters for year (an int) and make and model (both Strings) would look like this:

```
public void setYear (int x)
{
 year = x;
}

public void setMake (String s)
{
make = s;
}

public void setModel (String s)
{
 model = s;
}
```

\ TOSTRING()

At this point our class has four instance variables, four constructors, and eight getter/setter methods. There is another utilitarian method that is useful to create for each of our classes—the *toString* method.

After an object is created, we may often want to print its contents on the console. This is especially useful for testing—when creating an object, you may want to verify that the object was created properly by printing some of its attribute values to the console.

A crude way of accomplishing this would be to use the getter methods you created to print the output, like putting this code in the *main* method in your Tester class:

```
public class Tester {
    public static void main(String[] args)
    {
    Car myCar = new Car(2013,"Ford","Mustang", "red");

      System.out.print(myCar.getYear() + " ");
      System.out.print(myCar.getMake() + " ");
      System.out.print(myCar.getModel() + " ");
      System.out.print(" Color: " myCar.getColor());

    }//end main
}//end class
```

What if we just printed the *myCar* object itself, like this:

```
System.out.print(myCar);
```

What would print in this case? The variable *myCar* refers to an instance of the Car class with values in each of its four attributes (which were passed into the constructor when the object was created.) When you print a reference to an object, the default behavior is to print the memory address where the object resides in RAM, so the output of executing the previous statement would be something like this:

```
Car@5e8fce95
```

The funny looking number/letter combination after the @ sign is a hexadecimal number that represents the memory address of the Car object. This demonstrates that the Car instance resides at a unique location in your computer's RAM (memory.) As a matter of fact, if you were to create three Car instances in the main method in your Tester class and print them:

```
Car c1 = new Car();
Car c2 = new Car();
Car c3 = new Car();
System.out.println("c1 is at " + c1);
System.out.println("c1 is at " + c2);
System.out.println("c1 is at " + c3);
```

The printed output would look something like this:

```
c1 is at Car@4b71bbc9
c2 is at Car@17dfafd1
c3 is at Car@3343c8b3
```

This demonstrates that each Car object is a unique instance located in its own specific location in memory. This default printing behavior for an object is not magic or even hidden behavior. There is a method built into Java that is responsible for printing this depiction of an object—that method is called *toString*.

The *toString* method is not actually hidden—it resides in a library class named *Object*. If you create a class without a *toString* method, the one from the class *Object* is used. This is due to a feature of the Java language called *inheritance*, which we'll explore more later.

Instead of using this default *toString* method, it's possible to create your own customized version of *toString* which prints out whatever you want to display when printing an instance of your class. Just create a method with the following signature and be sure it returns a String:

```
public String toString()
{
    return "some String representation of your object";
}
```

Usually, we want our *toString* method to return a String containing some concatenated combination of values of an object's attributes. For our Car objects, we'd likely want to include year, make, model and color. To accomplish this, we could create the following *toString* method in our *Car* class:

```
public String toString()
{
    return color + " " + year + " " + make + " " + model;
}
```

So now, our Tester class could look more like this:

```
public class Tester {
    public static void main(String[] args)
    {
    Car myCar = new Car(2013,"Ford","Mustang", "red");
    System.out.print(myCar);
    }//end main
}//end class
```

And the output would now look like this:

```
red 2013 Ford Mustang
```

It's usually helpful to create a *toString* method for each class you create. This definitely helps with testing, but could also be useful anywhere else in your program where you need to see details of an object you created.

MODELING OBJECTS IN UML

Over the years there have been several ways to describe a software program before writing it. One of the oldest of these is pseudo code—a narrative description of an algorithm to be developed. There have also been several methods for describing software graphically. An old practice that is still in use is called a "flow chart." Others include data flow diagrams and entity relationship diagrams. These are primarily used with structured non-object oriented systems.

When the popularity of object oriented programming increased dramatically in the 1990s there were many books on the subject, and many of the authors of those books created new notational methods for describing software. At that time, software developers flocked in many different directions toward notations they had a preference for. This resulted in competing and conflicting notations. This became confusing—much like working in the United Nations, where many different languages are spoken. Many companies chose a standard notation to be used internally, but that didn't solve the industry-wide inconsistency problem.

There was a compelling need for one common notation that everyone in the software industry used. A standards setting body called the Object Management Group, or OMG, sent out a request for proposal (RFP) seeking submissions to be selected as the one standard notation. There were several proposals sent to the OMG to be considered as the standard, including some by large companies like IBM and Microsoft.

One of those submissions was presented by three of the popular object oriented programming authors who chose to collaborate. Jim Rumbaugh, Grady Booch, and Ivar Jacobsen combined the best elements of their notations into a single notation they called *The Unified Modeling Language*, or *UML*. After some back and forth discussion with the OMG, Rumbaugh, Booch, and Jacobsen (referred to my many as the "Three Amigos") heeded the OMG's guidance and incorporated some elements from other submissions. The result was a standard modeling language that is still the standard software modeling language used today.

As an introduction to one of the most commonly used components of the UML, we will learn how to create and use a model that describes the *structure* of an object-oriented system. This structural model is referred to as a class diagram.

Each Java class in a class diagram is represented by a three compartment box.

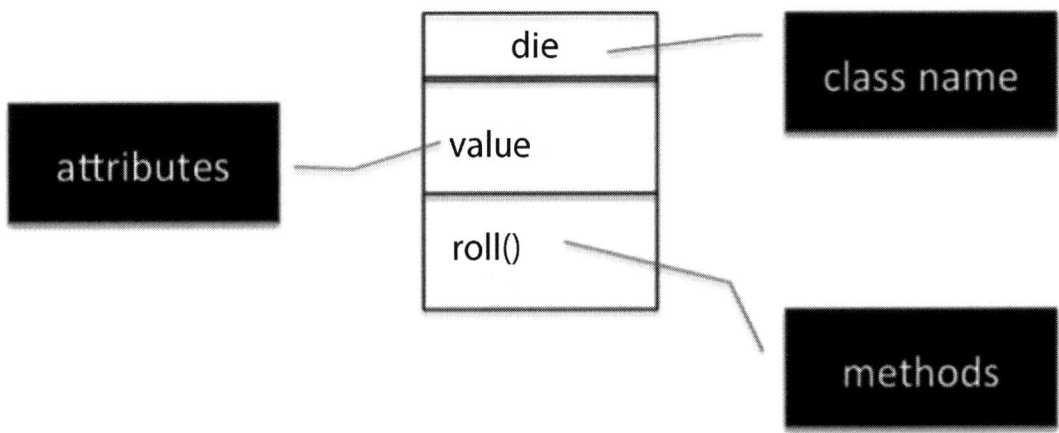

In the top compartment, the class name is capitalized and centered. In the middle compartment, the attributes (instance variables) are listed, and in the bottom compartment, the class's methods are listed. The diagram of the class *Die* above shows a simple UML representation of this class.

It can be helpful to a software developer if additional details about the attributes and methods are also included. For each attribute, we depict that the attribute will be declared as private by prefixing the attribute name with a minus sign (-). Additionally, we show the type (primitive or reference type) that the attribute will contain by putting a colon (:) followed by the type at the end of the variable name:

```
-value : int
```

For methods, we prefix the method name with a plus sign (+) to depict that it will be declared as public. If a method will have parameters, include the type of each parameter (without a variable name) inside the parentheses. If there are multiple parameters, each should be separated by a comma. Finally, at the end of the method name we put a colon (:) followed by the return type of the method (or *void* if the method won't return anything:

```
+roll()  :  int
```

Here is the detailed UML representation of our simple *Die* class:

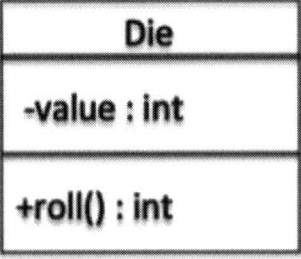

Here is a UML depiction of the *Car* class we created earlier with all notational adornments:

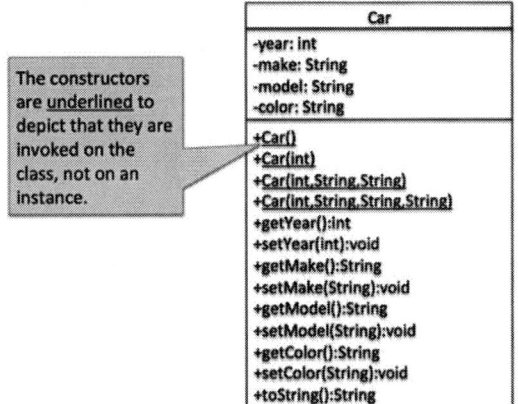

The constructors are underlined to depict that they are invoked on the class, not on an instance.

The complete Java class created from this model:

```java
public class Car
{
//Instance variable declarations
    private int year;
    private String make;
    private String model;
    private String color;

//Constructors
        public Car() {
        year = 1900;
        make = "Unknown";
        model = "Unknown";
        color = "Unknown"; }

        public Car(int x) {
        year = x;
        make = "Unknown";
        model = "Unknown";
        color = "Unknown"; }

        public Car(int x, String a, String b) {
        year = x;
        make = a;
        model = b;
        color = "Unknown"; }

        public Car(int x, String a, String b, String c) {
        year = x;
        make = a;
        model = b;
        color = c; }
```

```
//getters
        public int getYear ()
        { return year; }

        public String getMake ()
        { return make;}

        public String getModel ()
        { return model;}

//setters
        public void setYear (int x)
        { year = x;}

        public void setMake (String s)
        { make = s;}

        public void setModel (String s)
        { model = s;}

//toString
        public String toString()
        {
        return color + " " + year + " " + make + " " + model;
        }
}//END CLASS
```

CONSTRUCTING AN OBJECT ORIENTED SYSTEM

Building a single class is fairly straightforward if the model provides the attributes, method signatures, and a description of what each method is supposed to do. The attributes we have depicted thus far are referred to as *simple attributes*, which are those that are declared as primitives or Strings.

When we want to connect instances from two classes together, we also need *reference attributes*. In UML, we depict connecting two classes together with an arrow. In the example below, we show a new class named *Radio*. The diagram depicts that each *Car* instance contains a reference to an instance of *Radio*.

Note the direction of the arrow and the number on each end of the line. So we can focus on the reference attribute, we'll simplify the model by excluding the methods in this example.

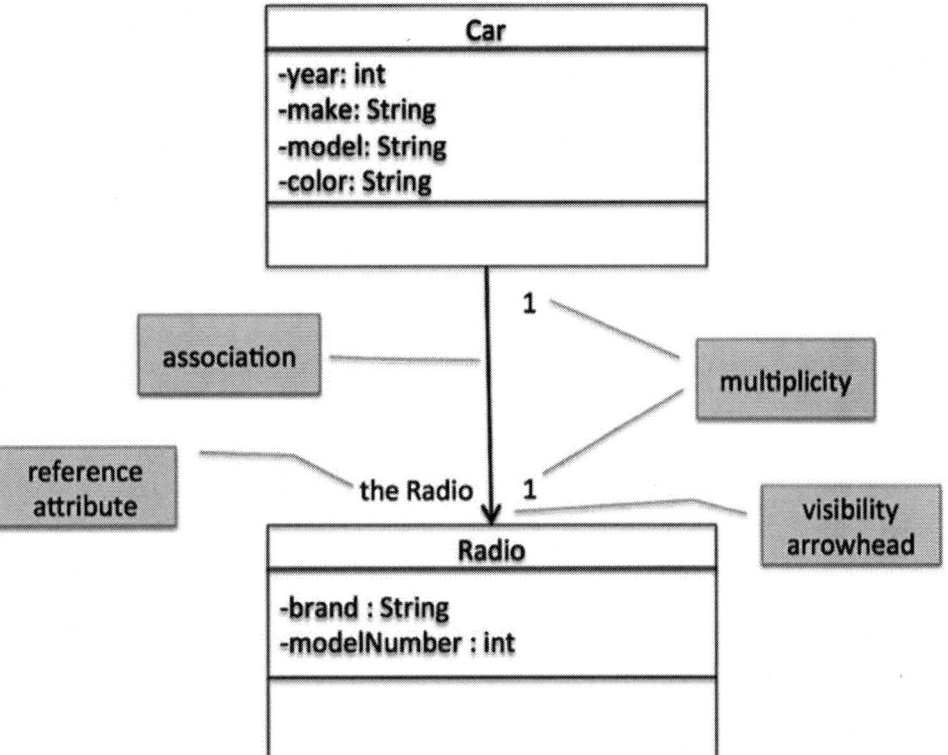

The numbers on each end of the line are called *multiplicity indicators*. We read this sample model:

> *Each Car object contains one Radio objects.*

AND   *Each Radio object is contained in one Car object.*

Think of this as *containment*—each *Car* objects **contains** a *Radio* object. However, containment doesn't work in reverse. A *Radio* object does not contain one *Car* object. The arrowhead indicates this. In a well-designed system, not only does an object contain instances of the class it is pointing to, but it is also the creator of those instances. This means that some method inside the Car class will contain Java code that creates one instance of the Radio class. When the *Radio* object is created, an additional attribute will be required in the Car class to retain its reference to the *Radio* object it created. This is called a *reference attribute*.

The name of the *reference attribute* is depicted in the diagram next to the arrowhead. The *reference attribute* becomes an instance variable in the class where the line with the arrow originates.

This means that in addition to its four simple attributes (year, make, model, and color) the class *Car* has a fifth attribute named *theRadio* which should be declared to contain a *Radio* object. The attribute declaration portion of the *Car* class now looks like this:

```
public class Car
{
 private int year;
 private String make;
 private String model;
 private String color;
 private Radio theRadio;
```

At this point, no Radio object has been created. A variable named *theRadio* has been declared as reference type *Radio* so it can eventually contain an instance of *Radio*.

Usually, the code to create the instances of reference variables is contained in a Constructor. Let's see what one of the constructors of our *Car* class might look like with this additional step:

```
public Car() {
  year = 1900;
  make = "Unknown";
  model = "Unknown";
  color = "Unknown";
  theRadio = new Radio();
}
```

What if an object needs to contain more than one of another object? In this case, the multiplicity indicator would be a number greater than one. In the model below, we'll add a reference from *Car* to four instances of *Tire*.

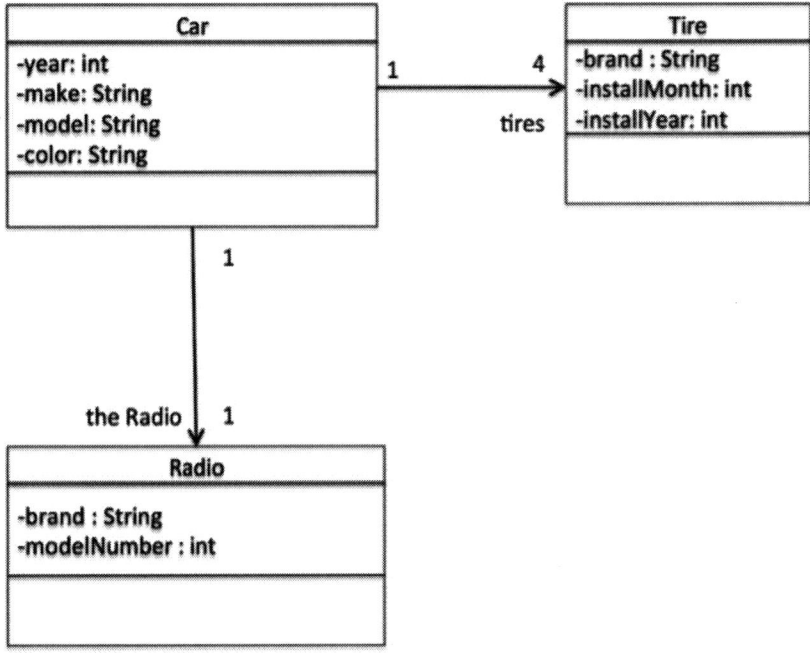

We would code this using the same approach we used for the *Radio*. A reference attribute named *tires* will need to be added to the *Car* class. A big difference with the *Tire* reference, however, is that there is more than one *Tire*. If the multiplicity indicator is greater than one, we will need to use an array to keep the four instances.

In this case, the variable *tires* in *Car* will be declared as an array of Tire objects. The Java code for this is:

```
public class Car
{
  private int year;
  private String make;
  private String model;
  private String color;
  private Radio theRadio;
  private Tire[] tires = new Tire[4];
```

For this example, we are not only declaring the private attribute *tires* as a *Tire* array, but we are also creating the *Tire* array of size four. Note that no *Tire* objects have been created yet. Just like the *Radio* instance, we would create the four *Tire* instances in a constructor and add each of them to the array:

```
public Car() {
  year = 1900;
  make = "Unknown";
  model = "Unknown";
  color = "Unknown";
  theRadio = new Radio();
  tires[0] = new Tire();
  tires[1] = new Tire();
  tires[2] = new Tire();
  tires[3] = new Tire();
}
```

Of course we would probably create constructors in *Radio* and *Tire* that would allow *Car* to pass in the initial values of their attributes, but we'll exclude that for now so we can focus attention creating the reference connection between two objects.

There are two other multiplicity values that can require different handling. When the multiplicity indicator is 1, we are saying that the *Car* must have one instance of *Radio*, no more, no less. The same is true for *Tire*: A *Car* must have four instances of *Tire* from the time it is created. To satisfy this, we create our *Radio* and *Tire* instances at the very beginning of creation of the *Car* instance. This is why we create these objects in the constructor. This ensures that when we invoke the *Car*'s constructor (e.g., *new Car()*), we know that the constructor will create those *Radio* and *Tire* instances.

When the multiplicity indicator is depicted as **0..1**, the reference variable exists in *Car*, but at any point in time that *Radio* instance may not exist. We use this for reference objects that we wish to create later in the program.

Finally, when the multiplicity indicator is depicted with an asterisk (*) the object contains zero to many instances of the referenced object. We use this when we don't know how many objects will be contained in the array.

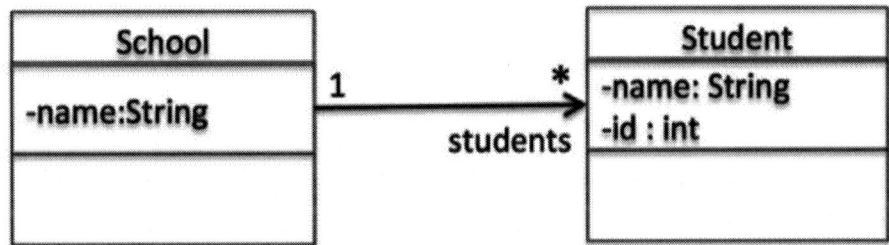

This poses a problem, however, because arrays are fixed size. Therefore, we would need to use something more elaborate than an array to handle the containment. In this situation, we could use an *ArrayList*, which allows us to handle variable sized containers. We'll skip this case for now, though, because we will be covering that later when we learn *ArrayLists*.

MODEL TO CODE IN EIGHT STEPS

Now that we've covered all the elements of building a Java system from a model, let's go back to the beginning and follow an 8-step process from model to code. For this example, we'll use a simplified representation of the model without all the adornments (private/public indicators, variable types, method return types, etc.) so you can focus attention on how to put a system together.

We will use the following model of a dice game which contains five classes and walk through each of the steps in building the Java code:

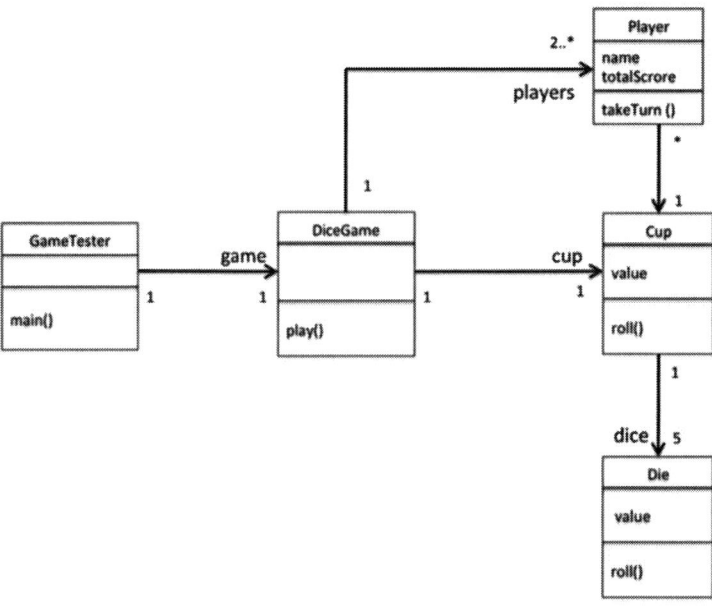

STEP 1: START AT THE "BOTTOM"

The first step is to figure out which of the five classes to build first. Since we now know that classes that have arrows pointing to other classes are going to be referencing and creating those objects. There is a dependency from the "pointing" class to the class being "pointed to." In this example, it would be impossible to fully build the *Cup* class if the *Die* class didn't exist yet.

So in this step, find a class in the model that has no outgoing arrows. It is completely independent and will not require that another class exists before it can be fully written and compiled.

In our example, *Die* is the only class that is independent, so we will build it first.

STEP 2: BUILD THE BASIC STRUCTURE OF THE CLASS

Simply get the class name from the model and build the Java shell for the class.

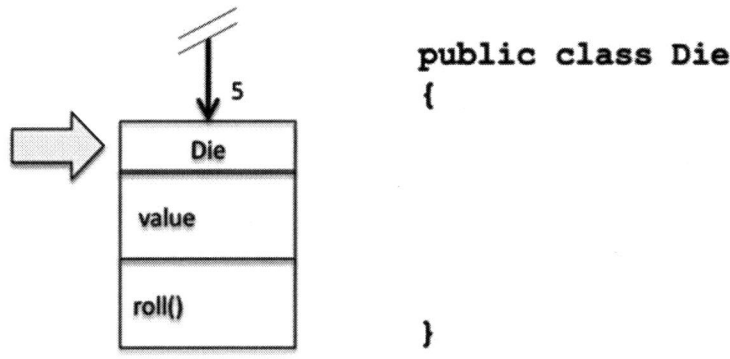

STEP 3: ADD THE SIMPLE ATTRIBUTES

Declare each of the simple attributes as private and with the appropriate type. If the type is not provided in the model, you must determine which type is best suited for the attribute. In most cases, these will be primitive types or Strings.

Put all the simple attribute declarations at the top of the class's block.

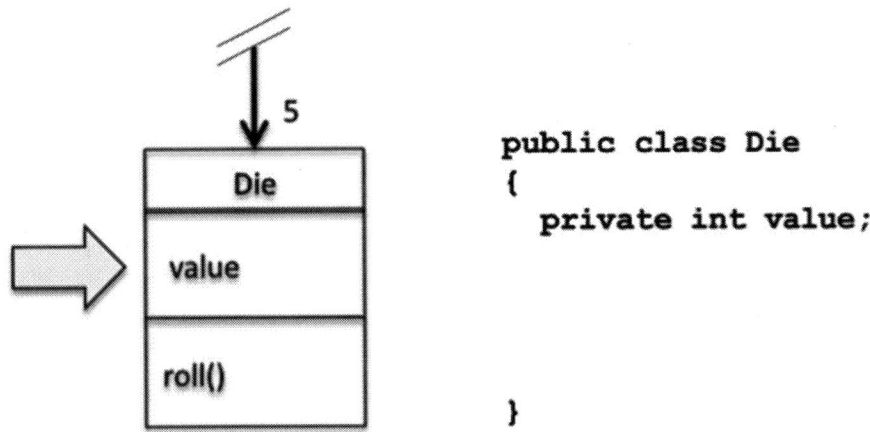

```
public class Die
{
    private int value;



}
```

STEP 4: ADD THE REFERENCE ATTRIBUTES

Declare each of the reference attributes as private and with the appropriate type. Our *Die* class has no outgoing arrows, so there are no reference attributes. Therefore, we would skip this step for the class *Die*.

Since we'll be repeating these eight steps for each of the classes on the model, let's look ahead at another class to see an example of adding reference attributes:

The class *DiceGame* has two outbound arrows, so it should have two reference attributes: *cup* which contains a single instance of the class *Cup*, and *players* which contains an array of *Player* instances.

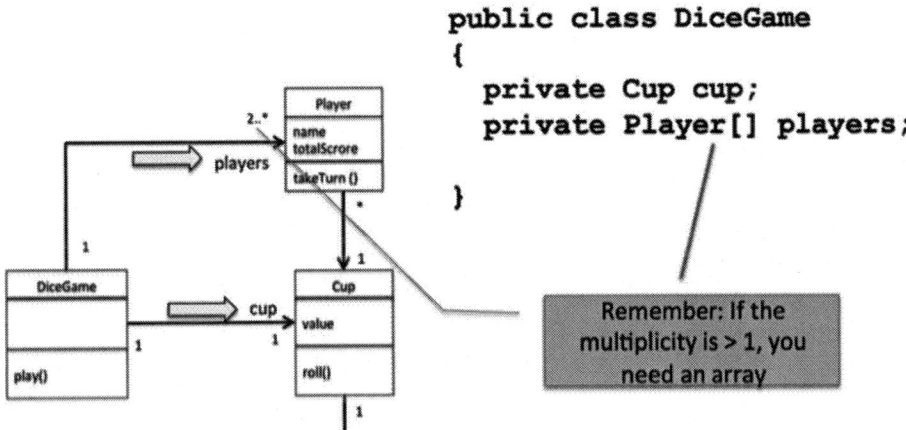

```
public class DiceGame
{
    private Cup cup;
    private Player[] players;

}
```

Remember: If the multiplicity is > 1, you need an array

As you can see, all the information needed to create the Java code can be found in the model. The only change you must make is to declare players as an array because the multiplicity indicator on the arrowhead is greater than one (2..*). Therefore, players should be declared as Player[], not Player.

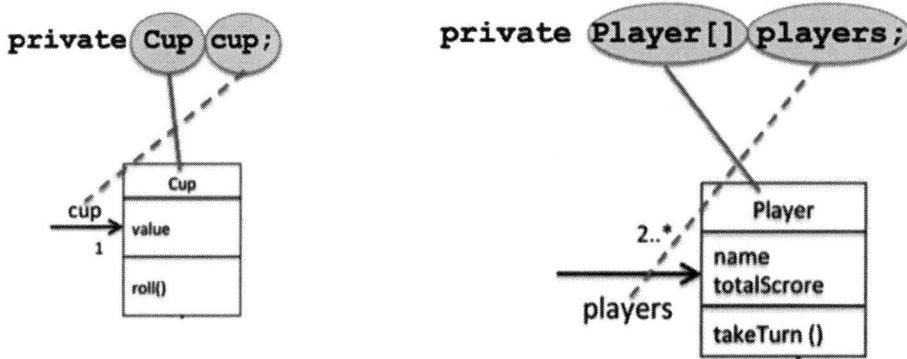

STEP 5: CREATE THE METHOD SIGNATURE AND BLOCK FOR EACH METHOD IN THE CLASS

The methods are listed in the bottom compartment of each three-compartment box. Use the information provided in the model to create the method signature. Most methods are declared as public. If the model doesn't provide the parameter types or return types, you will need to determine those things when writing the method. For now, just create a placeholder for the method and fill in its logic in a later step.

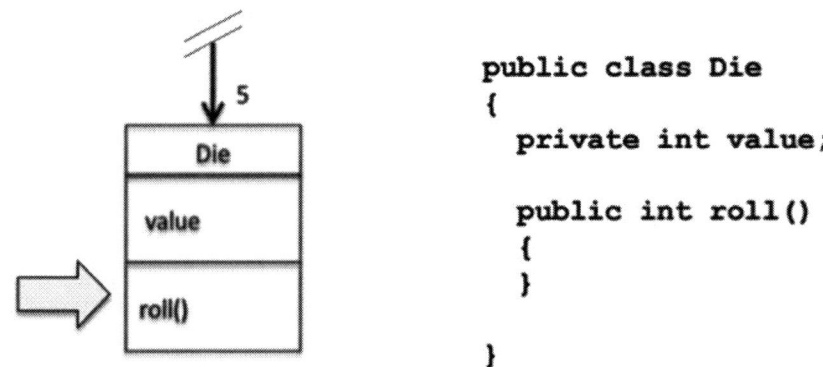

```
public class Die
{
    private int value;

    public int roll()
    {
    }

}
```

STEP 6: CREATE CONSTRUCTORS

If you don't create a constructor, a default (invisible) constructor will automatically be created for you. Since the behavior of the default constructor is often insufficient, it's a good idea to create your own constructor (or multiple constructors) for each class in your system.

The model may or may not include constructor names. Whether or not they are shown in the model, you'll need to determine what behavior makes sense within your constructor(s).

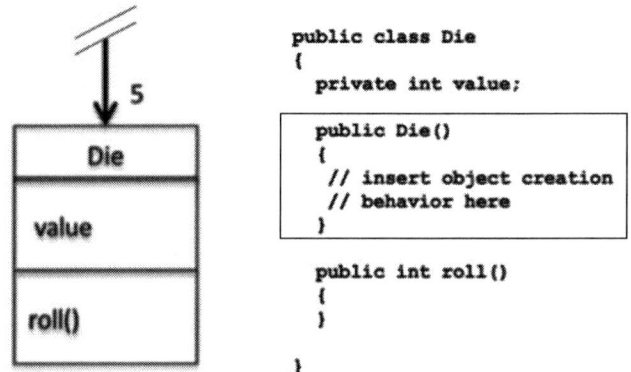

```
public class Die
{
    private int value;

    public Die()
    {
    // insert object creation
    // behavior here
    }

    public int roll()
    {
    }

}
```

STEP 7: CREATE THE TOSTRING METHOD

If you don't create a toString method, the default behavior when printing an object is to print its class name and memory address. It is usually helpful to create a *toString* method that includes information about the object such the values stored in some of its attributes.

When you create a *toString* method, make sure it has a return type of *String*, and include a return statement that returns a String representation of the object.

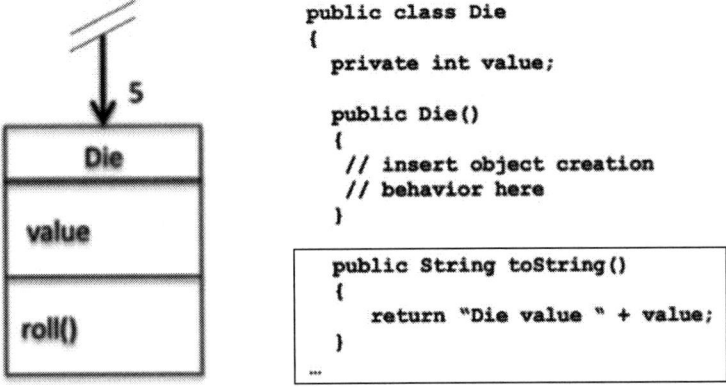

```java
public class Die
{
    private int value;

    public Die()
    {
        // insert object creation
        // behavior here
    }

    public String toString()
    {
        return "Die value " + value;
    }
    ...
```

STEP 8: FILL IN THE LOGIC IN THE INCOMPLETE METHODS FROM STEP 5

Each method in your model has a unique responsibility that must be coded in Java. Using your documentation, notes, pseudo code, and other requirements information, write the content of each of the methods you "stubbed out" in step 5.

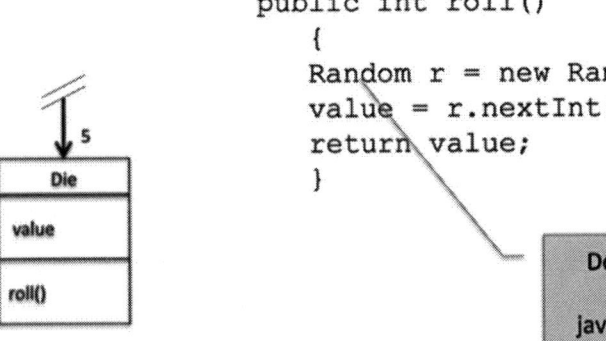

```java
public int roll()
{
    Random r = new Random();
    value = r.nextInt(6) + 1;
    return value;
}
```

Don't forget to import java.util.Random

REPEAT: Return to step 1 and select the next class to take through the 8 steps

Bear in mind that you are building one class at a time, and that as you build the 2nd class and beyond, expect to use reference attributes to "connect" your objects together.

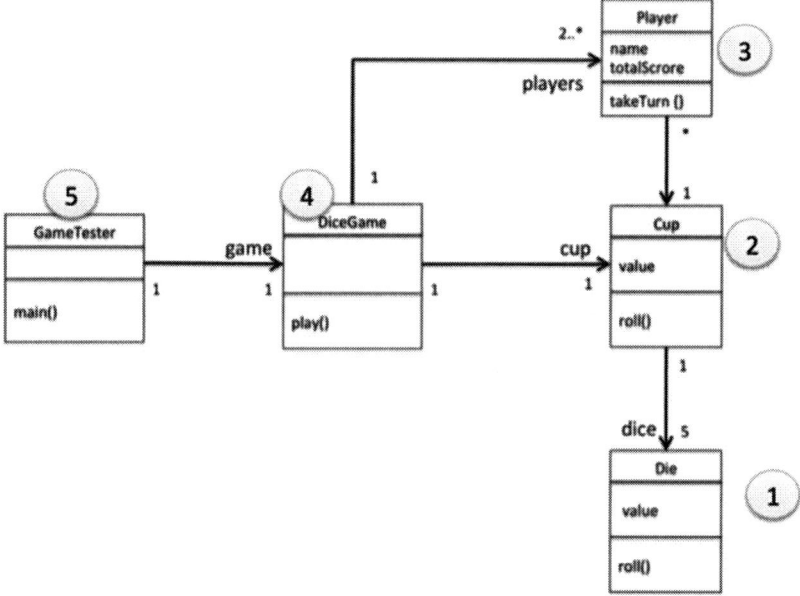

CHAPTER 7

COMPOSITION WITH ARRAYLIST

We have already learned about composition, or containment, where one object contains references to one or more instances of another class. We also learned that if an object references more than one instance of another class, we must use an array to contain those referenced objects. Arrays have limitations, though. In this chapter, we'll learn about a more elegant way of handling composition with a library class called *ArrayList*.

LIMITATIONS OF ARRAYS

Creating and using an array is fairly straightforward. Recall the simple way we create an int array when we know its contents in advance, using an array initializer:

```
int[] oddNumbers = {12, 3, 50, 7, 99};
```

This is a convenient way to quickly create a container with a small number of elements. The fundamental limitation of an array, however, is that it has a fixed size. The array above has a size of five, which cannot shrink or grow. If you create an array to contain ints that you'll populate later, you create the array like this:

```
int[] myNumbers = new int[?];
```

In place of the question mark, we substitute the size of the array. The problem is, if we don't know how many numbers we will need to store, it's difficult to specify the size of the array.

One crude solution to this is to make the array bigger than we think it may ever need to be:

```
int[] myNumbers = new int[1000];
```

This approach presents at last three problems:

1. We could guess wrong. What if it turns out we'll need to store 1500 ints?
2. It's wasteful: If we only need space for 10 ints now, we're wasting the space that's set aside for the other 90 elements.
3. A primitive array sets a default value for each element, so the slots we're not using will initially be set to zero. We could confuse this to be a data value that we previously set rather than an empty placeholder for future data.

A BETTER WAY

The *java.util* package contains several library classes in the *collection* category. These classes are specifically designed to maintain *variably sized* homogeneous collections of objects.

Homogeneous means that collections must contain objects of the same type. This is the same restriction that arrays have.

Variably sized means that a new collection starts at size 0 and grows as we add elements to it. If we remove elements from the collection, the size shrinks. This is very efficient—a collection will always be precisely the size we need it to be at that time.

The only feature of arrays that is not supported by collections is the handling of primitives. An array can contain primitive elements, but a collection cannot. A collection can only contain objects. This is why we didn't introduction collections until after starting object oriented programming.

THE COLLECTIONS FRAMEWORK

A collection is an object that often referred to as a data structure, which exists for the purpose of containing references to other objects. A collection represents a group of objects, known as its elements. Some preserve the order of the elements in the collection, while others do not. The specific type of collection you choose to create will be based on criteria like these.

There are several library classes in *java.util* that are part of the collections framework. Here is a comparison of three uniquely different types:

ArrayLIst	Maintains the order in which you put elements in the collection. For example, when you add a new object to an ArrayList, they are always placed at the end of the list. If you remove an element from the middle of the list, the ArrayList size shrinks by one, but the order of its elements is still preserved.
HashSet	The Set collection types prevent duplicates. If you try adding the same object to a HashSet more than once, it will only retain one reference. To manage this, the HashSet keeps the elements in its own order, so there is no guarantee that it will retain the order that you add elements to this type of collection.
HashMap	Maintains key/value pairs. For example, studentID may be a key, and a Student instance could be the object paired up with that key. Each key value must be unique.

For now, we'll focus on *ArrayList*. It is the most general purpose of the collection types, and will satisfy most of our needs.

CREATING AN ARRAYLIST

Because the ArrayList is homogeneous, when we declare and create one, we must specify what type of object it will contain. We do this using a new syntax format we haven't seen before:

```
ArrayList<Type> arrayListName = new ArrayList<Type>();
```

The <Type> constrains the ArrayList to contain only elements of the specified type. For example, if we wanted to create an ArrayList named *students*, which only contains instances of the class *Student*, we would do the following:

```
ArrayList<Student> students = new ArrayList<Student>();
```

The easiest way to make sure you handle the syntax properly, is to make sure you always include the type contained within the < and > characters. This concept is called *generics* in Java. Look carefully at the syntax above. Note that the declaration of the variable students is simply ArrayList with the suffix <Student> on the tail end of the name. On the right side of the assignment statement, the ArrayList constructor includes the same suffix. Just don't forget to include the parentheses with the constructor on the right hand side.

ADDING ELEMENTS TO AN ARRAYLIST

Once we have created an ArrayList, its initial size is always zero. To add elements to the ArrayList instance, simply send the add message to it, passing along the object you want to add. Make sure the object you pass with an *add* message is of the <Type> you specified when declaring and creating the ArrayList. The following will create two instances of Student then add them to the *students* ArrayList we created above:

```
Student s1 = new Student(12345,"Fred Jones");
Student s2 = new Student (23456,"Mary Smith");
students.add(s1 ) ;
students.add(s2 ) ;
```

Of course, we could have done this more efficiently by bypassing the temporary variables s1 and s2:

```
students.add( new Student(12345,"Fred Jones") );
students.add( new Student (23456,"Mary Smith") );
```

RETRIEVING ELEMENTS FROM AN ARRAYLIST

An object can be retrieved from an ArrayList using its index location and the *get(int)* method:

```
Student s = students.get(0); //retrieves the Student at index location 0
```

This could potentially have undesirable results, however. Because ArrayLists can shrink and grown, it's possible that there is no object at any given index location. If you were to try to retrieve an object from an nonexistent index location, you will receive an "index out of bounds exception" when you run the program.

```
Student s = students.get(99); //Index out of bounds exception
```

The use of *get* to retrieve all objects in an *ArrayList* works well if you create a loop and set the upper bounds of the loop as the size of the array. The size of the array (its total number of elements) can be determined by sending the *size()* message to an ArrayList object.:

```
int x = students.size(); //sets x to the total number of objects in students
```

Using *size()*, we can create a loop to extract all elements of the ArrayList as follows:

```
for(int c = 0; c < students.size(); c++ _
    System.out.println("Student: " + students.get(c) );
```

Make note of the fact that there are no square brackets when dealing with the ArrayList. Instead of *students[c]*, which we would have used with an array, we use *students.get(c)* to retrieve the object at index location c.

Just as with arrays, we can retrieve all elements of an ArrayList using the abbreviated *for* loop:

```
for(Student aStudent : students)
    System.out.println("Student: " + aStudent);
```

USEFUL ARRAYLIST METHODS

Here is a summary of methods that can be used with an ArrayList:

add(anObject)	Adds an object at the end of the ArrayList
clear()	Removes all objects from the ArrayList
contains(anObject)	Returns *true* if the object is contained in the ArrayLIst, if not, it returns *false*
get(int)	Return the object at the specified index location
indexOf(anObject)	Returns an *int* with the index location of *anObject*
remove(anObject)	removes the first occurrence of *anObject*
remove(int)	removes the object at the specified index location
size()	returns an *int* with the total number of objects in the ArrayList

ARRAYLIST PRACTICE

Let's explore a Java solution to a simple two-class model. PigPen contains 10 instances of the class Pig.

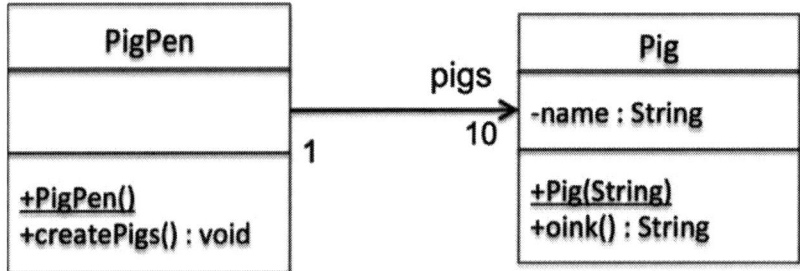

If we were to use a standard array to implement containment in the model below, the code for PigPen would look like this:

```
public class PigPen
{
private Pig[] pigs = new Pig[10]; //Fixed size array to contain 10 Pigs

public PigPen()
{createPigs(); }

public void createPigs()
{
pigs[0] = new Pig("Porky");
pigs[1] = new Pig("Wilbur");
pigs[2] = new Pig("Babe");
//etc...

}//end method createPigs


}//end class PigPen
```

This solution is limiting, though, because we must create an array of size 10, which could be too big or too small. For flexibility, we'll eliminate the fixed size of the list, and we'll use an ArrayList instead of an array:

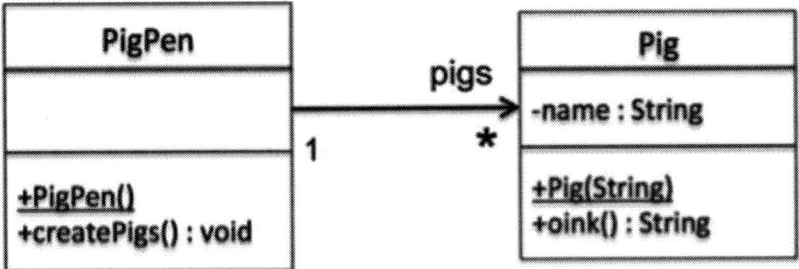

The implementation of PigPen would change to the following:

```java
import java.util.ArrayList; //We MUST import the ArrayList class

public class PigPen
{

private ArrayList<Pig> pigs = new ArrayList<Pig>() ;

public PigPen()
{ createPigs(); }

public void createPigs()
{
  pigs.add(new Pig("Porky"));
  pigs.add(new Pig("Wilbur"));
  pigs.add(new Pig("Babe") );
//etc…

}//end method createPigs

}//end class PigPen
```

With this approach, our collection can be sized based on the number of Pig objects that is added to the ArrayList. It won't be any smaller or larger than it needs to be.

CHAPTER 8
INHERITANCE

A very powerful and useful feature of object oriented programming languages is implementation of a concept called *Inheritance*. To understand the benefits of inheritance, it's usually best to think of it as *specialization*.

ABSTRACTION

Take a look at the following pictures, and organize them into groups of your choosing:

© VLADJ55, 2013. Used under license from Shutterstock, Inc.

© alexmisu, 2013. Used under license from Shutterstock, Inc.

© imging, 2013. Used under license from Shutterstock, Inc.

© Scott Prokop, 2013. Used under license from Shutterstock, Inc.

© Patryk Kosmider, 2013. Used under license from Shutterstock, Inc.

© Konstantin L, 2013. Used under license from Shutterstock, Inc.

© angelo sarnacchiaro, 2013. Used under license from Shutterstock, Inc.

© alexmisu, 2013. Used under license from Shutterstock, Inc.

There are numerous ways that these buildings could be classified, with no clear right or wrong approach. It's possible to create a single classification called "building" and put all the structures in that single category. Alternately, they could be categorized by size: big buildings, medium-sized buildings, small buildings. This would require some specification of dimensions for each of the categories.

Another approach is to categorize the buildings by usage: churches, offices, and residences. The process of looking at a collection of things and finding the common attributes or behaviors they all share is called abstraction. In software development, abstraction is useful for classification of types when designing a system.

In the building examples above, you may have noticed that some buildings were easier to categorize than others. Buildings that have the same attributes (i.e. the information that describes it) can fall into the same category. For example, a church may have a steeple, while all residences have a kitchen. This is often not enough, though. For example, it's common for churches not to have steeples, and for offices (and churches for that matter) to have kitchens. When classifying types in a system, we may consider attributes, but we may also consider behavior—in other words, what would each building be used for?

In UML, we depict specialization as a hierarchy of classes using an open triangle pointing from a specialized sub-type to its more generalized super-type. Here is a depiction of building classification. Note that church is broken down into another level of specialization:

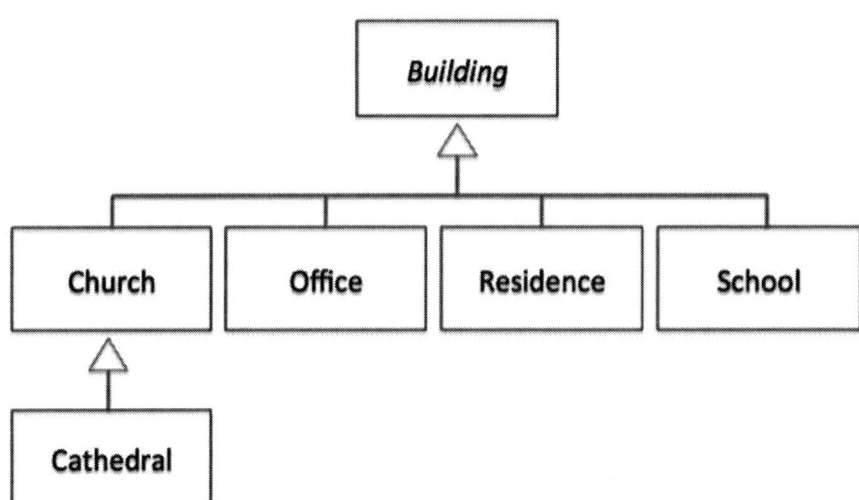

AN EXAMPLE OF SPECIALIZATION WITH SOFTWARE

Let's look at an example of specialization with a Die. Recall that when we created a Die object and sent it the message *roll()*, the sending of the message caused the Die object we sent the message to execute its *roll* method.

Let's introduce another class called *LoadedDie*, which appears to be very similar to a *RegularDie*. A *LoadedDie* object has built-in bias: The loaded side is rolled approximately 50% of the time, and 50% of the time one of the other five sides is rolled.

Think of these concepts (*RegularDie* and *LoadedDie*) as two different "flavors" or specialized types of *Die*. Depicted in the Venn diagram below, read it as the inner type "is a" outer type. In other words, a *RegularDie* is-a Die and a *LoadedDie* is-a Die. Everything you can say about a *Die* applies to a *RegularDie* and to a *LoadedDie*.

Therefore, if we can *roll* a *Die* object, we should be able to *roll* a *RegularDie* or a *LoadedDie*.

If we were to fill a cup with *Die* objects, and we didn't know whether they were instances of *RegularDie* or *LoadedDie*, we could still shake the cup and *roll* all of the Die objects it contains. By shaking and emptying the cup, we are essentially sending the *roll* message to each of the *Die* objects it contains. We need not concern ourselves with each separate *Die* or worry about what specialized type of Die each one happens to be.

When we roll all the dice in the cup, each Die will handle its own behavior by implementing its own version of the *roll* method. The *RegularDie* objects will generate a fair random number from 1 to 6, and the *LoadedDie* objects will generate a biased roll based on its loaded side. The one sending the roll message doesn't even need to know which types of Die are contained in the cup. This demonstrates an object-oriented concept called *polymorphism*. *Polymorphism* means "One message, different behaviors."

MORE ABOUT INHERITANCE

Inheritance is primarily about creating classifications of types that have shared characteristics. In the field of Biology, we classify species based on common attributes and/or behaviors.

For example, there are lot of types of reptile in the animal kingdom such as lizards, alligators, turtles, and snakes. Each of these species is quite different from one another, yet they all share that they are cold-blooded, have bodies covered with scales, shields or plates, and have offspring born in eggs with a hard outer shell.

In software, this classification system helps group classes together that have shared attributes and/or behavior. This not only reduces the amount of code we need to write, but it actually makes our system easier to maintain and enhance, as we will illustrate in this chapter.

MORE ABOUT POLYMORPHISM

Let's look at an example of specialization with animals. Let's create different types of Animal (e.g., Dog and Cat) and give each the ability to respond to the message "talk()." By setting up Dog and Cat as subtypes of Animal, and by implementing the "talk()" method in Animal, it becomes safe to send the *talk()* message to any type of Animal.

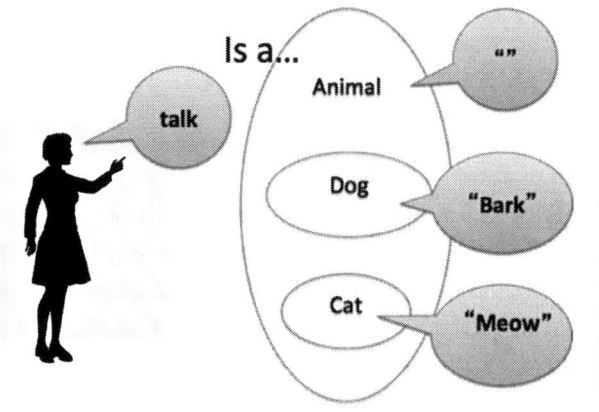

If the message is sent to a *Dog*, it says "Bark!". If the message is sent to a *Cat*, it says "Meow!". However, if I send the message *talk()* to another *Animal* object that is neither a Dog or a Cat, it says nothing. The *talk()* method in the class *Animal* has a default behavior of saying nothing so that is the behavior that will occur when sending the *talk()* message to any *Animal* that isn't a *Dog* or a *Cat*.

To emphasize the point, imagine a cage full of different animals. All you know is that all animals can respond to the message "talk," but you don't have to know how each different type of animal implements talking. A dog will bark, a cat will meow, a lion will roar, a giraffe will make no sounds, etc. Essentially, *polymorphism* makes the sender of the message's life easier.

BACK TO THE DIE

Looking at the RegularDie, let's depict its contents using UML:

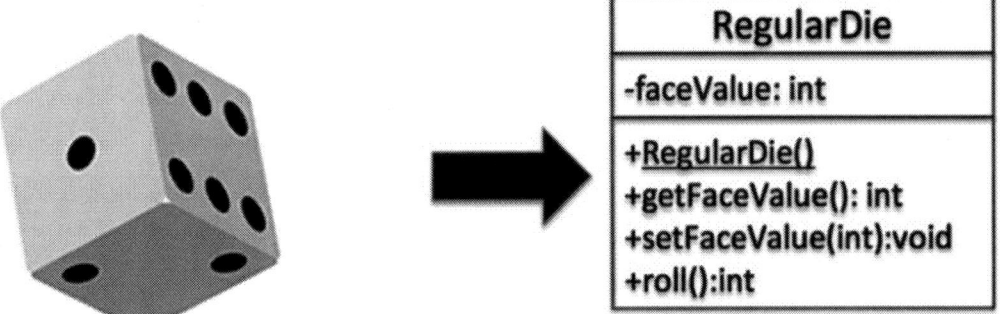

Now, let's depict the LoadedDie:

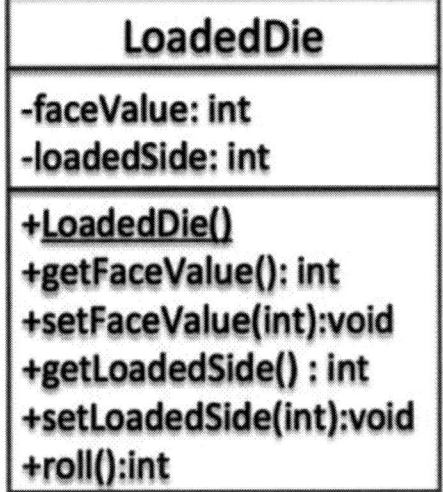

When we put these two classes side-by-side, note the similarities and differences:

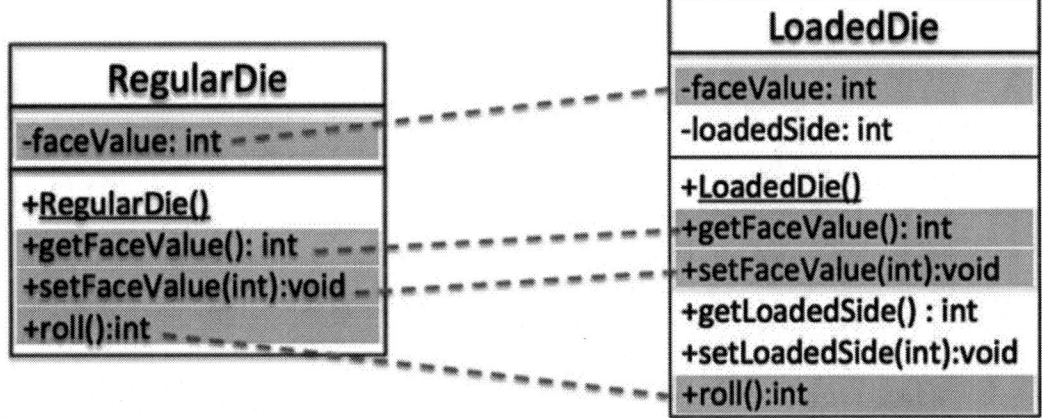

We can eliminate the redundancy by combining these two classes into a single class hierarchy. Note the open triangle notation. This indicates that *LoadedDie* is a subclass of *RegularDie*:

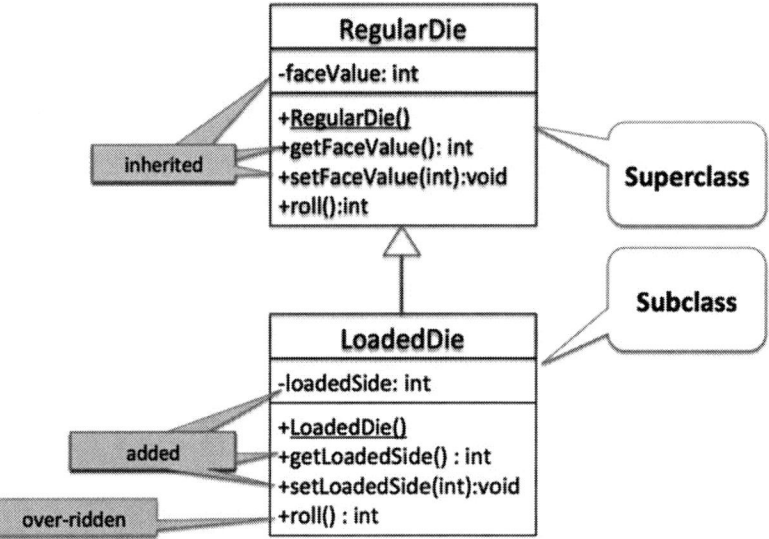

To implement this, we introduce the Java keyword *extends*. The class signature of *LoadedDie* would look like this:

```
public class LoadedDie extends RegularDie
{
}
```

At this point, the keyword *extends* causes *LoadedDie* to automatically *inherit* the attribute *faceValue* and the methods *getFaceValue, setFaceValue, and roll*. It does not, however, inherit the constructor *RegularDie()*.

The only additional code required in *LoadedDie* are attributes and methods that we are adding to the functionality it inherits from *Die*, AND any methods it inherits from *RegularDie* but that it wishes to *override*. Here is the complete code for the class *LoadedDie:*

```
//import the Random class, which is needed in the roll method
import java.util.Random;

public class LoadedDie extends RegularDie
{
      //added attribute:
      private int loadedSide;

      //added methods:
      public int getLoadedSide() { return loadedSide; }
      public void setLoadedSide(int x) { loadedSide = x; }

      //overridden (changed) method:
      public int roll()
      {
      Random r = new Random();
      if(r.nextBoolean())
            return loadedSize;
      else
            return r.nextInt(6) + 1;

      }//end roll method

}//end class
```

◠POLYMORPHIC DICE

As mentioned earlier, polymorphism makes the sender of a message's life easier. Imagine throwing a bunch of Die objects into a cup, shaking them, and rolling them. If you are the one rolling all these dice, you don't want to have to worry about giving each Die specific instructions how to do its job. If the cup of dice contains a mixture of RegularDie and LoadedDie objects, each will take responsibility for its own rolling behavior due to polymorphism.

To further illustrate this in Java, let's make two enhancements to our system. First, let's create a new Die class called *Die* that both *RegularDie* and *LoadedDie* are subclasses of. We'll move all attributes and methods that are shared by both subclasses up to the *Die* class:

While we're at it, let's add another type of Die, a *TenSidedDie*, which returns a random value between one and ten. Using the Venn diagram depiction we used earlier, our *Die* types now look like this:

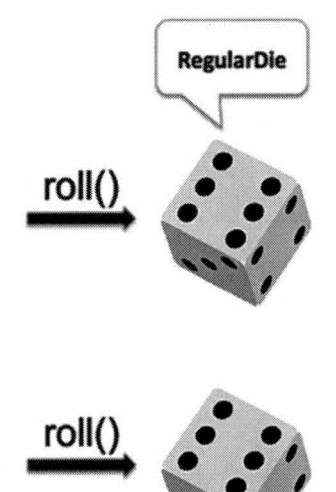

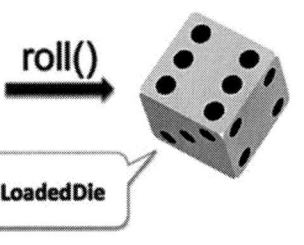

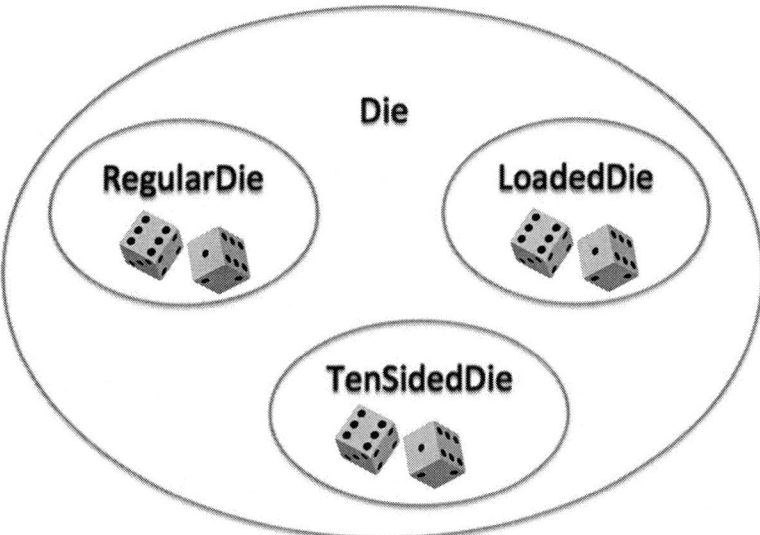

Let's now assume that all Die objects that we'll need will always be either a *RegularDie*, a *TenSidedDie*, or a *LoadedDie*. If this were the case, what is the purpose of the *Die* classification? *Die* is an abstraction of the other three sub-types of *Die*. In the real world, we use this solely for classification (descriptive) purposes. In software, however, we can use this abstraction to contain attributes and methods that are shared by all its subtypes.

In Java, we can create a class called *Die* and declare it as *abstract*. By declaring a class as *abstract*, we prevent it from being instantiated. Any attempt to create a *new Die()* will result in a compilation error. So if we can't create an instance of a *Die*, what is the purpose of creating an abstract class? It exists solely for the purpose of providing attributes and methods that are inherited by its subclasses.

In UML, we depict an abstract class by italicizing its name. Let's see what our four *Die* classes now look like in UML:

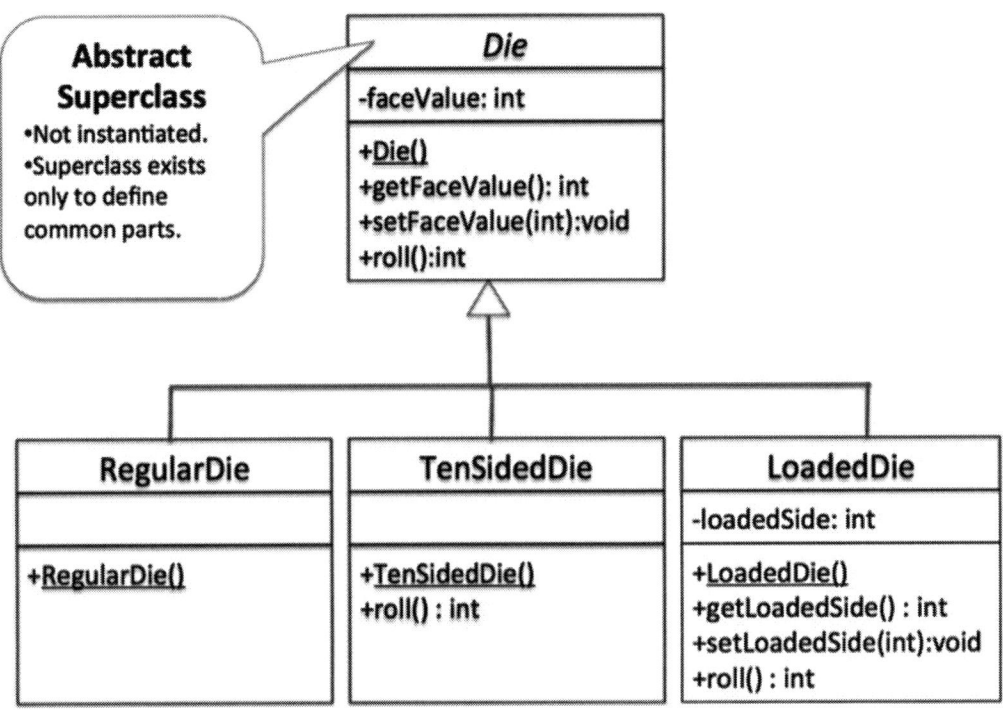

CONSTRUCTORS AND INHERITANCE

Simply put, each class must have its own constructor. Constructors from a superclass aren't inherited. Because a subclass is a specialization of its superclass, it's conventional for the first line of the constructor of a subclass to make a call to the superclass constructor. We do this using the Java keyword *super*. The keyword *super* is followed by a set of parentheses that may or may not contain parameters—based on the format of the superclass constructor.

In our *Die* example, the class *RegularDie* will have its own constructor which makes a call to the constructor in class *Die* (its superclass) as follows:

```
public class RegularDie extends Die
{

    public RegularDie()
    {
    super(); //calls the constructor in class Die

    }

}
```

We would do the same with the constructors in *TenSidedDie* and *LoadedDie*.

```
public class TenSidedDie extends Die
{

    public TenSidedDie()
    {
    super(); //calls the constructor in class Die
    }
```

```
        //insert overridden roll() method

}

public class LoadedDie extends Die
{

        private int loadedSide;

        public LoadedDie()
        {
        super(); //calls the constructor in class Die
        }

        //insert overridden roll() method, loadedSide methods, etc.

}
```

So what about the superclass that all three of those classes inherits from? It should be declared as *abstract* to block it from being instantiated.

```
        public abstract class Die
        {

                private int faceValue;

                public int getFaceValue() { return faceValue; }
                public void setFaceValue(int x) { faceValue = x; }

                public int roll()
                {
                Random r = new Random();
                return r.nextInt(6) + 1;
                }//end roll method

        }//end class
```

ATTRIBUTE ACCESS MODIFIERS AND INHERITANCE

Up to now we have always declared our methods as public and attributes (instance variables) as private. We learned that by declaring an instance variable as private, we enforce encapsulation. This means that the only place that the value of an attribute can be changed or retrieved is within some method within the same class.

With inheritance, this can become an inconvenience. In our sample problem, it's not possible to access (or change) the value of the attribute *faceValue* in any of the methods of *RegularDie*, *TenSidedDie*, or *LoadedDie*. This attribute is private in the abstract superclass *Die*, and it can only be accessed by methods in that class. This is true even though the attribute and methods from *Die* are all inherited. This can cause confusion to those who are new to object oriented programming.

The reason for this is actually sound—any changes to the definition of the attribute *faceValue* in *Die* could potentially require changes to methods that use (or change) the contents of that attribute. Since the attribute is *private*, we are guaranteed that no method in any class other than *Die* do not contain code that uses this attribute directly. This reduces the maintenance burden of our system, and is a major benefit of encapsulation.

Often, though, we would like to relax that encapsulation enforcement a bit when we are inheriting an attribute. To accomplish this, Java offers an access modifier called *protected*, which is halfway between *private* and *public*. When an attribute is declared as *protected*, it can be accessed/changed only by methods within its own class, or within methods of its subclasses. By changing the access modifier of *faceValue*, this attribute can now be used directly by methods in any of the three subclasses of *Die*:

```
public abstract class Die
{
        protected int faceValue;

        // rest of the class Die

}//end class
```

INHERITING TOSTRING

You have actually been using inheritance ever since you started using object-oriented programming. When you declare a class without using the *extend* keyword, you are actually automatically extending a library class called *Object* by default. This means that you always inherit all the methods from *java.lang.Object* in every class you create. One of those methods is *toString()*. The *toString()* method in *java.lang.Object* will return a String containing the name of the class followed by the hexadecimal memory address of the object.

When we create a *toString()* method in the classes we create, we are actually *overriding* the *toString()* method that we have inherited.

ANOTHER EXAMPLE

In this example, we have two concrete classes: Person and Student. (Concrete means that neither class is declared as abstract, and each of these classes can be instantiated.)

Let's look at the superclass (base class) first. The class *Person* has one attribute: *name*. We have a getter and setter for that attribute, as well as two constructors.

One constructor sets the name to a default value, and the other constructor accepts an incoming String to set the name's value to.

The *toString* method will simply return the name of the Person object that it represents.

That leaves one (slightly) more complex method: *sameName*. This method compares the name of another *Person* object passed to it and returns *true* if the names match, or *false* if the names don't match.

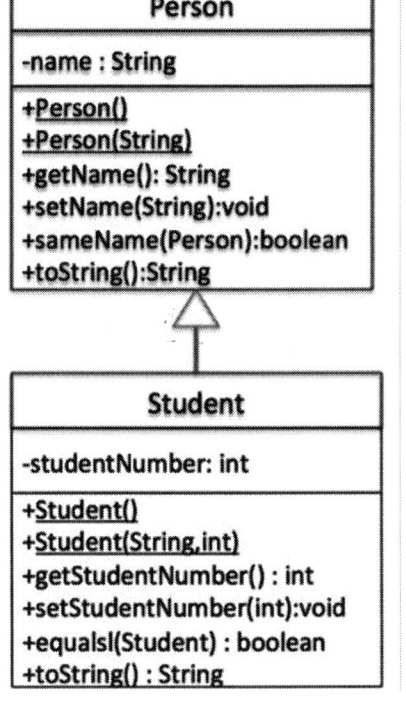

Let's look at the Java code for the *Person* class:

```
public class Person
{
  private String name;

public Person() //Constructor with no name passed to it
  {
    name = "No name yet.";
  }
```

```java
public Person(String initialName) // Constructor with name passed in
 { name = initialName; }

//getter and setter
public void setName(String newName) { name = newName; }
public String getName() { return name; }

//override default toString
public toString () { return "Person: " + name; }

public boolean sameName(Person otherPerson) {
  return (this.name.equalsIgnoreCase(otherPerson.name));
  }//end method sameName
}//end class Person
```

Now let's look at the Java code for the subclass *Student*:

```java
public class Student extends Person
   {
     private int studentNumber;

     public Student() {
   super();//Call the superclass constructor before anything else!
   studentNumber = 0;//Indicating no number yet
   }

public Student(String initialName, int initialStudentNumber)
   {
   super(initialName); //pass the first value up to the superclass constructor
   studentNumber = initialStudentNumber;
   }

public int getStudentNumber() { return studentNumber; }
public void setStudentNumber(int newStudentNumber)
   { studentNumber = newStudentNumber; }

public String toString() {
   return super.toString() + " Student Number : " +   studentNumber;
   }

public boolean equals(Student otherStudent) {
   return (this.sameName(otherStudent)
     && (this.studentNumber == otherStudent.studentNumber));
   }//end method equals
}//end class Student
```

So now let's create a testing class with a main method to create a Student object and test out this code:

```
public class InheritanceDemo
{
  public static void main(String[] args)
  {

  Student s = new Student();
  s.setName("Warren Peace");
  //setName is inherited from the class Person.
  s.setStudentNumber(2013);
  s.writeOutput();
  }
}
```

The output from running this should be:

Name: Warren Peace
Student Number: 2013

CHAPTER 9

FILE I/O

So far, every program we have written has either had hard-coded data compiled in your program code (which would rarely if ever happen in the real world) or we entered data from the keyboard at runtime (using the Scanner). Most programs that manipulate data, however, require a permanent way to save data for future use. In this chapter we learn how to perform basic file input/output (file I/O) in Java.

MEMORY AND DATA

Recall that if you were to turn off your computer's power, only information stored in secondary memory is retained. Examples of secondary memory are your hard drive, solid state drive, USB stick, CD, DVD, etc.

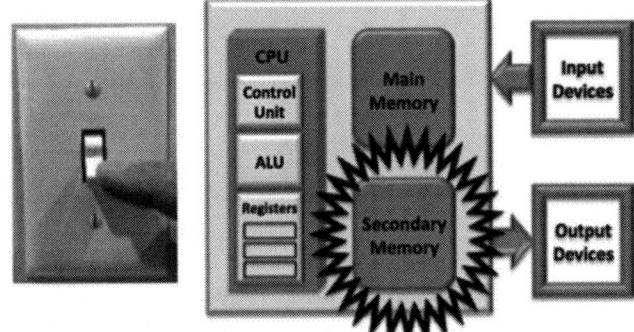

To retain and use data each time we run our program, we need a way to save data captured and/or manipulated in our program to secondary memory. We also need a way to read data saved in secondary memory back into our program. To do this, we will use library classes to help perform file I/O functions.

DATA STREAMS

File I/O uses the concept of streaming. To understand streaming, consider the way a water pipe works. Water enters one end of the pipe and flow through until it exits the other end of the pipe. If you were able to trace a water molecules as they make their journey through the pipe, you would expect each molecule to exit the pipe in the same order that they entered.

Data streaming occurs the same way. When we stream data into from an external text file into our program, we read in and process one byte at a time. The same process occurs when we stream data out to an external file.

When streaming in data from an external text file, Java relies on the underlying operating system to let it know when it has reached the end of the file. Each operating system (e.g., Windows, Mac OSX, etc.) manages the placement of an invisible end-of-file marker whenever a new file is created.

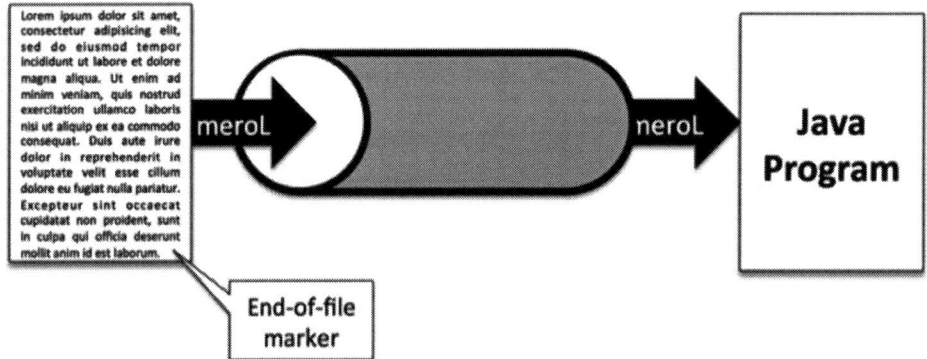

When streaming in the data one byte at a time, streaming terminates as soon as that end-of-file marker is reached. Conversely, when streaming data out to an external file, the operating system will insert an end-of-file marker at the end of the file after you notify it that you are done streaming.

CREATING A TEXT FILE WITH FORMATTER

The library class *Formatter* is used to create an external text file, and can be found in the *java.util* package. There are five steps to writing a text file using *Formatter*:

1. Import the class.
2. Support Java exception handling.
3. Create an instance of Formatter and associate it with an external file name.
4. Write out a stream of data (may include a loop to stream multiple chunks of data).
5. Close the file to notify the operating system to place the end-of-file marker.

1. IMPORT THE CLASS

The *Formatter* class is found in *java.util*. Import it above the class signature:

```
import java.util.Formatter;
```

2. SUPPORT JAVA EXCEPTION HANDLING

We will cover exception handling in more detail later in the chapter. For now, just know that we cannot compile a program that contains and file processing without including exception handling code. At this point, we'll practice using a single class with a *main* method, and we can handle this simply by inserting *throws Exception* at the end of our *main* method signature:

```
public static void main(String[] args) throws Exception
```

3. CREATE FORMATTER INSTANCE

Inside the *main* method, create an instance of *Formatter*. The *Formatter* constructor requires a String containing the name of the external text file we will be creating (e.g., "output.txt").

```
Formatter f = new Formatter("output.txt");
```

At this point, the stream has been opened to write to this file, but no file has actually been created yet. If you are using the command line to execute your program, the default location for the file we create is the same folder where our .class file resides. If you are using Eclipse, the file will be saved in the parent folder that contains the *bin* and *source* files. Here is a Mac example. If we were to create our sample program in the Spring2013 project, the output file will be written in the Spring2013 folder within the Eclipse workspace folder:

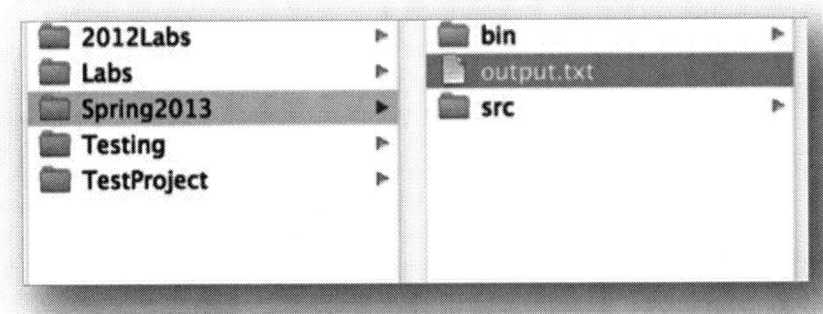

If you want your file to be written somewhere else, you can include the complete folder hierarchy within the String containing the file name. This is often referred to as the file's *path*. For example, in Windows, if you want to create the file on your computer's *C* drive in a folder named *data*, you would open the *Formatter* as follows:

```
Formatter myFormatter = new Formatter("c:\data\output.txt");
```

On the Mac, specifying folder names works a little differently. The "/" character at the beginning of a file name always refers to the root directory on your Mac. Note that it slants the opposite direction of the directory symbol on Windows. If you open a Terminal window and type "cd /", it will take you to the root directory. You can then use "*cd foldername*" to navigate down to the folder where you want to save your file. This example shows writing the folder on my desktop:

```
Formatter myFormatter = new Formatter("/users/ken/desktop/file.txt");
```

4. WRITE OUT A STREAM OF DATA

The *Formatter* class has a method named *format* that is used to write out a stream of data to your output file. The *format* method supports the same substitution characters as the *printf* method. The most straightforward use of *format* is to simply pass it a String:

```
myFormatter.format("text that will be written to my file");
```

With substitution symbols, just use the same syntax you learned for *printf*:

```
myFormatter.format("%s that will be written to %s","text","my file");
```

You can continue to send multiple format messages in your program until you have written all the data you wish to include in your output file. The *format* method does not insert any carriage returns, so the stream will continue across the first line. If you want to write data to separate lines, just include the "\n" escape sequence inside the String that you pass to *format*:

```
myFormatter.format("line1 still on line 1\nline2\n");
```

This would produce the following output:

```
line1 still on line 1
line2
```

5. CLOSE THE FILE

To notify the operating system that you are done writing to the file, send the *close* message to your *Formatter*. At that point, an end-of-file marker will be inserted at the end of your file. The *close* message has no parameters:

```
myFormatter.close();
```

When the file has been closed, it is available to open and view/edit using a text editor or word processor. It's also available to read back into your program, which we'll learn how to do next. If you don't close your output file, it will be left in a state of limbo and will be unusable, so this step is very important.

A COMPLETE EXAMPLE

The following program shows the use of all five steps to write out a text file that includes a header on the first line followed by all the odd numbers from 1 to 99 on the second line:

```
import java.util.Formatter;

public class TestIO
{
public static void main(String[] args) throws Exception
{
Formatter f = new Formatter("file.txt");
f.format("Odd Numbers:\n");
for(int i = 1; i <= 99; i++)
  f.format("%d ", i);
f.close();
}
}
```

BEYOND THE BASICS

Each time you open a Formatter, write data to the output file, and close it, the previous contents of the file (if it already exists) are wiped out and replaced with the new content. There are ways to append an existing file, but this requires the use of additional library classes and methods, and we're going to focus on this basic approach at this time.

BINARY FILES

Additionally, the file we wrote is a standard text file. Basically, this means that it's human readable. You can open it with a standard text editor (Mac textedit or Windows notepad) and read/edit the contents. Most word processors like Microsoft Word also support reading in data from a text file.

There is a more efficient way to store data in files – the binary file format. When you write to a binary file, it cannot be opened with a standard text editor. The data is converted to a compressed binary format when it is written. This allows us to store data in smaller files. This also requires additional Java classes and methods that is beyond the scope of this chapter. We must use these same Java classes to read data back into our program from a binary file. This is the approach that is typically used by commercial software applications when you save data. If you were to try to open a PowerPoint file using a text editor, it will attempt to load the data in the text editor, but it's not human readable and won't appear to make any sense.

READING IN A TEXT FILE WITH SCANNER

We have been using the library class *Scanner* to capture data typed into the keyboard by the user of our program as follows:

```
Scanner myScanner = new Scanner(System.in);
int x = myScanner.nextInt();
```

We are going to use this same library class to read in data from a text file. To do this, we will need to change the parameter of *Scanner*'s constructor. Instead of *System.in*, which represents the keyboard, we will pass *Scanner* a reference to an existing external data file.

First, we must import the *Scanner* class, as we have done before. We must also import the *File* class from the *java.io* library:

```
import java.util.Scanner;
import java.io.File;
```

Inside a method within our class, we next create an instance of *File*, passing a String to its constructor using the same file naming approach we used with *Formatter*. When reading in from a text file, it's very important to include the correct path name so your program is able to find the file.

If you run the program and the file can't be found in the folder you specify, your program will throw an Exception and exit. (We'll cover Exception handling later in this chapter.) Incidentally, your program will still compile okay if the file/path names are wrong because the compiler doesn't check to see if the file is there.

This will create a *File* object to read in a file named "data.txt":

```
File myFile = new File("data.txt");
```

We have used *Scanner* in the past without having to deal with Exception Handling, but creating this *File* object requires us to support it. For now, just add *throws Exception* at the tail end of your method signature:

```
public static void main(String[] args) throws Exception
```

Now, once the *File* object is created, we can pass it as the parameter to our *Scanner*'s constructor:

```
Scanner input = new Scanner(myFile);
```

Next, we can read in data from the file using all the same *Scanner* methods we've used before:

```
input.next();       //reads in the next String, up to the first space it finds
input.nextLine();   //reads in the next complete line as a String
input.nextInt();    //reads in the next item as an int
input.nextDouble(); //reads in the next item as a double
```

When using *Scanner* with the keyboard, your user enters one piece of data at a time. When using *Scanner* with streaming, it continues to read each *next* method reads in data from the stream until it encounters a delimiter, which by default is a blank space. This means that you need to be careful when creating your input file to ensure that its data is in the same sequence that your program will be reading it in.

The methods *next()* and *nextLine()* are mostly foolproof, because they will treat anything contained in your file as a *String*. The *nextInt()* and *nextDouble()* methods, however, will stumble if the next chunk of data does not match its type.

Let's say our data file has the following contents:

```
United States of America 1776
```

If our first line of code is *nextInt()*, our program would throw an Exception and exit, because we're trying to convert the String "United" to an int. If instead, we do the following:

```
String myString = input.nextLine();
```

The *String* named myString contains the entire contents of the line: "United States of America 1776."

If we use *next()*:

```
String myString = input.next();
```

The contents of *myString* will be "United." The *next()* method reads from the current spot up to the first space it encounters, because a blank space is the default delimiter used by Scanner.

To read in the first four *Strings* as a single *String*, we would need to use four *next()* messages (or create a loop that sends the *next()* message four times in a row):

```
String myString = input.next();
myString += input.next();
myString += input.next();
myString += input.next();
```

Each time you send a subsequent *next* method to the Scanner, it skips over the blank spaces and resumes reading at the next character it encounters.

At this point, it's possible to read in the next value "1776" as an integer:

```
int year = input.nextInt();
```

DELIMITERS

Delimiters are data separators in our data file. As mentioned, the default delimiter used by *Scanner* is the blank space. When you send a *next* message to your *Scanner*, very blank space it encounters is skipped over until it reaches the next non-space character.

What if you want to include a spaces as part of the data you are importing? The new line / carriage return is also treated as spaces are treated. If you put each chunk of data on a separate line in your data file and read in each line using *nextLine()*, you will get the entire contents of the line. Let's change our data file to this:

```
United States of America 1776
```

```
String myString = input.nextLine();
```

The value of *myString* now contains "United States of America."

It's also possible to change the delimiter character that the *Scanner* uses to separate data by sending the message *useDelimiter* to the *Scanner* object. The following will set the comma character as our delimiter:

```
input.useDelimiter(",");
```

Now if we change our data file to:

```
United States of America 1776
```

The space is no longer a delimiter, so the first *next()* message will read in "United States of America." It will then skip over the comma and resume reading at the next character.

Be careful! When we set the delimiter to comma, each space is treated as a readable character in the stream. If we were to follow our previous *next()* message with a *nextInt()*, we would get a runtime exception because there is a blank space in front of 1776, and *Scanner* is going to try to read it in as an int. In this situation, you'll want to clean up the data file and eliminate the unnecessary spaces.

CLOSE

Before ending your program, you must close the file. If you don't it will remain in limbo and you won't be able to access or use it in your program or other programs.

To close the file, simply send the *close()* message to the *Scanner*:

```
input.close();
```

A COMPLETE EXAMPLE

The following example shows opening an external text file, reading in a *String* and an *int* that are separated by a comma in the data file, then prints out the values:

```
import java.util.Scanner;
import java.io.File;

public class TestIO {
public static void main(String[] args) throws Exception
{
  Scanner input = new Scanner(new File("data.txt"));
  input.useDelimiter(",");
  String myString = input.next();
  int x = input.nextInt();
  System.out.printf("File contained %s and %d",myString, x);
  input.close();}
}
```

⟍EXCEPTION HANDLING

Now let's get back to why we needed *"throws Exception"* at the end of our method signature. Think back to the first programs you wrote. Your first learning "battle" was to overcome syntax errors. If you made a capitalization error or forgot a semicolon, the Java compiler was unforgiving. You weren't able to successfully compile your program until all syntax errors were found.

In addition to Java syntax errors (punctuation, capitalization, keyword violation, etc.) the Java compiler also checks for a few other things that it knows are guaranteed to make your program fail. For example, if you make a reference another Java class that hasn't been imported or doesn't exist in the same package, the compile will fail.

There are other problems, however, that the compiler is unable to detect. While the compiler checks every individual part of your program, it doesn't execute the logic within your program. Problems that occur within the program logic during the execution of your program are referred to as *Runtime Exceptions*.

The following logic will compile, but will fail during runtime:

```java
int[] nums = {1, 3, 5, 7};
int max = 10;
for(int x = 0 ; x < max ; x++)
   System.out.println(nums[x]);
```

The counter within this loop is being used to access an index location in the array *nums*. The array has a size of 4, so it's highest index location is 3. As soon as the loop counter reaches 4 and we try to print nums[4], the program will fail. When you run the program you'll see the following output:

```
1
3
5
7
Exception in thread "main" java.lang.ArrayIndexOutOfBoundsException: 4
      at TestIO.main(TestIO.java:8)
```

As you can see, the program successfully runs and prints out values until it reaches the invalid index location. At that point, the JVM displays a meaningful message to help you diagnose the problem, notably: *ArrayIndexOutOfBoundsException*. The compiler couldn't have possibly predicted this problem without executing the program logic, which it doesn't do.

Of course, in this particular program, it would make better sense to change the value of the variable *max*. However, what if the value of *max* was entered by a user or passed in by another object? In this case we couldn't know if the array bounds will be exceeded until the program is run.

Instead of accepting the JVM's default behavior when this *Exception* occurs, you could write code that executes if this Exception were to occur. We do this using a *try..catch* block.

First, create a try block surrounding the logic where the *Exception* could occur:

```java
int[] nums = {1, 3, 5, 7};
int max = 10;
```

```java
try {
      for(int x = 0 ; x < max ; x++)
        System.out.println(nums[x]);
} //end try block
```

A *try* block requires a corresponding *catch* block. The *catch* block has a single parameter which contains a reference to an Exception object that will be passed to it by the JVM. Without a *try* block, when a runtime exception occurs, the JVM catches the exception and terminates your program. If the exception occurs inside a *try* block, however, flow control continues in the corresponding *catch* block. If we wanted to print a friendly message and not exit the program, we could do the following;

```
public class TestIO
{
public static void main(String[] args) throws Exception
{

  int[] nums = {1, 3, 5, 7};
  int max = 10;
  try {
  for(int x = 0 ; x < max ; x++)
   System.out.println(nums[x]);
  }
  catch (ArrayIndexOutOfBoundsException e)
  {
  System.out.printf("Array boundary exceeded. Max = %d is too large\n",max);
  }
}//end main method
}//end class TestIO
```

The library class *ArrayIndexOutOfBoundsException* is one of several subclasses of the library class *RuntimeException*, which the JVM catches during runtime when they occur. These Exception classes are in the *java.lang* library, so it's not necessary to import them.

It's possible that more than one type of exception could occur in your program. Another common exception is an *ArithmeticException*, such as dividing by zero. Without a *try..catch* block, the following code would terminate your program and throw an *ArithmeticException:*

```
int x = 5;
int y = 0;
int result = x / y;
```

So we could avoid the termination of our program by putting the logic inside a *try* block:

```
try {
int x = 5;
int y = 0;
int result = x / y;
}
catch(ArithmeticException e)
{
System.out.println("Math problem!");
}
```

What if we wanted to combine the array code and the math code within the same *try* block? In this case, we would need to catch either of two possible types of exception, an *ArrayIndexOutOFBoundsException* or an *ArithmeticException*. So which do we put as the parameter of the *catch* block?

One approach would be to climb the hierarchy and catch a generic *Exception*, like this:

```
catch (Exception e)
{
System.out.println("Something bad happened!");
}
```

This will prevent the program from terminating, but the message isn't very helpful. Which problem occurred? This isn't just about printing a meaning message. When an exception is caught, we're likely going to want to execute some code that rectifies the problem. When we catch a generic *Exception* like this, we wouldn't know which problem to fix.

A more helpful approach is to catch both exception types. Each *try* block can have multiple corresponding *catch* blocks. When an exception is thrown at runtime, the first caught exception will jump to its corresponding catch block, skipping over the remainder of the code within the *try* block.

```
int[] nums = {1, 3, 5, 7};
int max = 10;
int x = 5;
int y = 0;
try {
int result = x / y;
for(int x = 0 ; x < max ; x++)
   System.out.println(nums[x]);
}
catch (ArrayIndexOutOfBoundsException e)
{
System.out.printf("Array boundary exceeded. Max = %d is too large\n",max);
}

catch(ArithmeticException e)
{
System.out.println("Math problem");
}
```

What if some other type of exception is thrown? It may not be necessary to create a *catch* block for every possible type of exception. Usually, programmers will include a generic catch block for everything they didn't already cover:

```
catch(Exception e)
{
System.out.println("Something else happened");
}
```

In addition to *try* and *catch*, you can also include an optional *finally* block at the end. The contents of the *finally* block are always executed no matter what happens inside the *try* block. Even if you choose to terminate your program inside one of your *catch* blocks, the code inside *finally* will execute before that happens.

```
finally {
System.out.println("Last but not least....finally!");
}
```

EXCEPTION HANDLING WITH FILE I/O

Programs that read and write text files are highly prone to exception situations. There are potential problems at runtime that are completely outside the control of the programmer, such as:

- Try opening an external text file that has been deleted or moved.
- Try creating/writing a file on a disc that is full.
- Try creating/writing a file in a secured folder without proper permissions.

As an example, If you try opening an external text file to stream contents into your Java program and the file is not where your program says it is, the JVM will throw a *FileNotFoundException*. If this situation were to happen, you would probably want to intercept the problem and handle it rather than have the program to exit.

When including an I/O related class such as *java.io.File* or *java.util.Formatter* in your program, the Java compiler is going to require you to handle the possibility of thrown exceptions when your program is running. You have two choices to satisfy this requirement:

1. In the signature of the method than contains your *File* and/or *Formatter* code, throw the caught *Exception* back to whoever called your method. This is the way we satisfied the exception handling requirement earlier in the chapter:

   ```
   public void myMethod() throws Exception { //method contents }
   ```

   PRO: It's quick and easy.

   CON: It's a punt. You are ignoring the potential problem and guaranteeing that the program will fail if a file I/O problem occurs.

2. Put the file I/O code inside a *try..catch* block:

   ```
   public void myMethod() {
           try {
           //code related to File or Formatter objects
           catch {Exception e}
           { // logic that responds to the exception}
   ```

   PRO: You can intercept the problem and do what we can to deal with it.

   CON: Requires a bit more planning and forethought about possible problems and what to do if they occur. Not all potential problems are resolvable.

FILE I/O AND OBJECT ORIENTED PROGRAMMING

All the examples in this chapter have used a single class with a *main* method. When constructing a system, most likely the file I/O code will be embedded far into your system in some method of some class that's called by an object, that's called by another object.

In the illustration below, if the file I/O logic is contained in the method labeled "3" in ObjectC, we could use the simple exception handling option and put *throws Exception* at the end of method 3's signature. If an exception occurs during program execution, method 3 will throw that exception back to the object that called it.

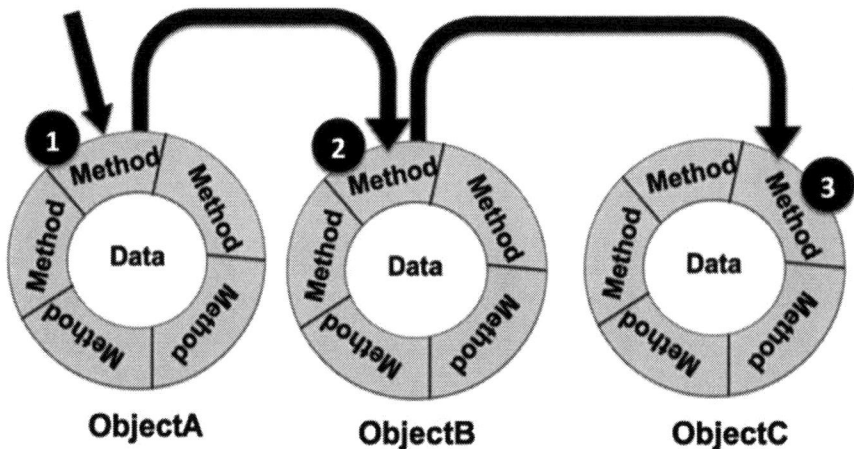

Since method 2 in ObjectB calls ObjectC's method 3, and because ObjectC's method 3 chose not to handle the exception, it now becomes the problem of ObjectB's method 2. Again, ObjectB's method 2 could simple be declared with "throws Exception" to push the problem back to ObjectA's method 1. If none of the objects/methods includes a *try..catch* block to handle the problem, we'll eventually end up back at our *main* method in the class where our system begins. If that *main* method also declares *throws Exception*, the JVM will intercept it and stop execution of the program.

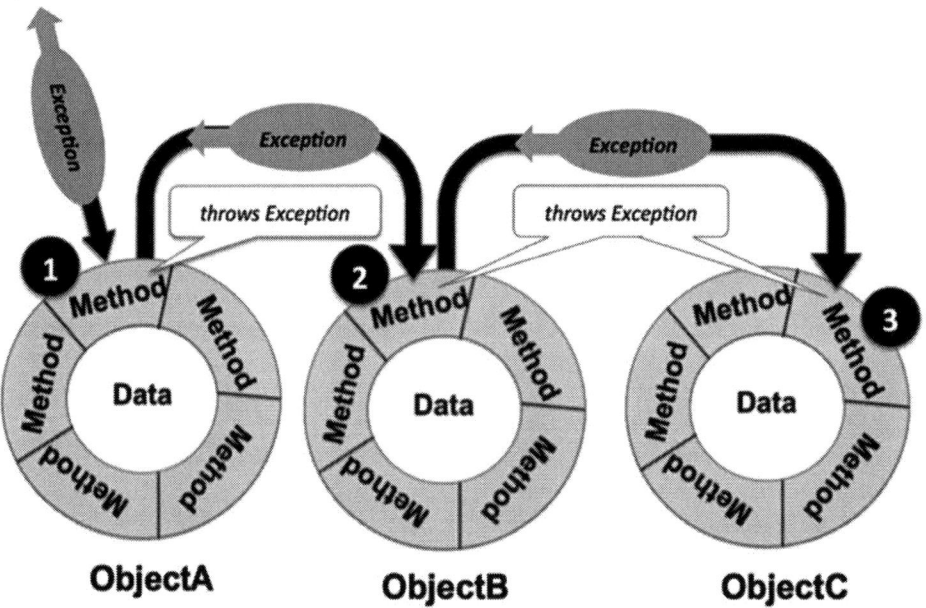

If on the other hand, ObjectC's method 3 includes a *try..catch* block, then ObjectB and ObjectC won't have to deal with any type of exception handling – it will completely be contained within and handled by *ObjectC*.

⟍ A COMPREHENSIVE EXAMPLE

To demonstrate both reading and writing to/from text files, we'll construct a simplistic little system comprised of a *School* containing a collection of *Student* instances. The *School* constructor will call its *loadStudents* method. In the *loadStudents* method, *Student* objects will be created by reading in a list of student names and id's from an external data file. When the *printRoster* message is sent to the *School*, it will write out an external file containing a roster of students.

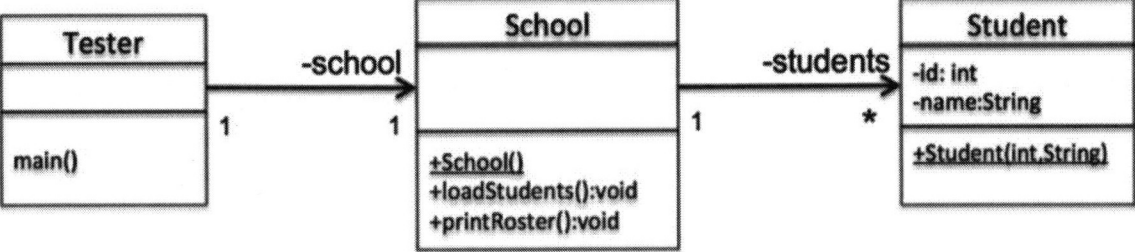

Let's start with the *Student* class. It simply has two attributes which are set to values passed into its constructor. We'll also include a *toString* method for our *Student*:

```
public class Student
{
private int id;
private String name;

  public Student(int x, String s)
  {
  id = x;
  name = s;
  }

  public String toString()
  {
   return "Student #" + id + " Name: " + name;
  }
}
```

The Tester class contains the main method which creates a *School* instance then sends it the *printRoster* message. We wouldn't be able to compile this one until we build the *School* class, but let's cover it now so we can focus on the file I/O logic inside the *School* class:

```
public class Tester
{
  public static void main(String[] args)
  {
  School s = new School();
  s.printRoster();
  }
}
```

Now let's look at the School class, where all the interesting things happen. Pay attention to the comments, which describe each part of the program. To run the program, you'll need to create the *students.txt* input file, which is described in the program comments:

```java
//Required to maintain the Student collection:
import java.util.ArrayList;

//Classes for importing from a text file:
import java.io.File;
import java.util.Scanner;

//Class for streaming out a text file:
import java.util.Formatter;

public class School
{

ArrayList<Student> students = new ArrayList<Student>();

public School()
{ loadStudents(); }

public void loadStudents()
{
//Create the Scanner and associate it with an existing
//external text file that contains student id's and names.
//The file will look like:
//11111,John Doe,22222,Mary Smith,33333,Pat TeeCake

try {
  Scanner input = new Scanner(new File("students.txt"));

  //Set the delimiter to a comma so we can include
  // spaces in student names:
  input.useDelimiter(",");

  while(input.hasNext())  //read until reach end-of-file
  {
   int a = input.nextInt();
   String s = input.next();
   Student aStudent = new Student(a,s);
   students.add(aStudent);
  }
  input.close(); //When finished, remember to close the input file
 }
catch(Exception e)
{ System.out.println("Problem reading input file"); }

}//end method loadStudents

public void printRoster()
{
 try {
```

```
      Formatter f = new Formatter("roster.txt");
      f.format("STUDENT ROSTER\n"); //print a header on the output file
      for(Student aStudent : students)
        {
            //write out one line per student:
            f.format("Student: %s \n", aStudent.toString());
        }
      f.close(); //When finished, remember to close the output file
}
catch(Exception e)
      { System.out.println("Problem writing output file"); }

} //end method printRoster

} //end class
```

CHAPTER 10

GRAPHICAL USER INTERFACES

All computer software requires at least some human intervention. While some programs may just need a kick start to run, other programs may require a lot of human intervention. Thus far, we have implemented user interaction with the *Scanner* (keyboard input) and *print*, *println*, and *printf* statements. This approach works fine for testing program functionality, but it's not <u>conventional</u> for a modern computer system. In this chapter, we'll learn how to create a graphical user interface (GUI) to interact with our application.

BUILDING IN LAYERS

Well designed systems are developed in "layers," where the classes that support the user interface are completely separated from the classes that represent what's referred to as the *domain*. For example, if we were building a point of sale system, we would start by building all the classes related to this domain, placing all the functionality related to each of these components in methods within the domain classes.

While constructing the domain classes, we may use the *Scanner* for keyboard input, and we may use *println* statements to display feedback on the console. This should be considered temporary, however, for testing and debugging our application.

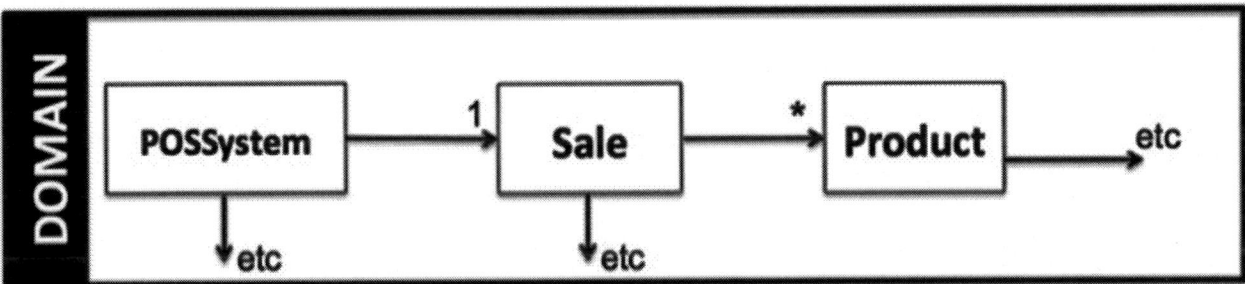

Following a layered approach to designing our application, it makes sense to break apart common services with the intent of containing the complexity of those services to a few classes. For example, inserting file I/O related logic in methods of several of our domain classes, remove it altogether from the domain layer. Instead, create a file handling class that manages all the file I/O complexity and exception handling. Our domain class would then interface with this file handler class whenever file handling is needed.

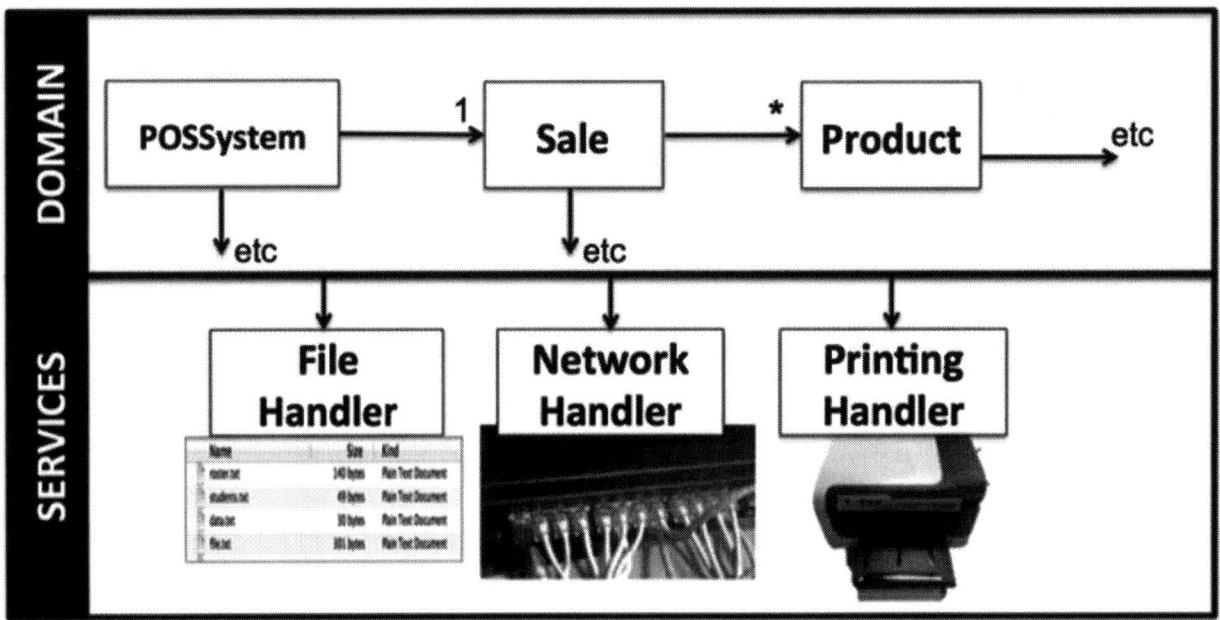

While this may require more abstraction in designing our file handling functionality, it can reduce the overall complexity of our application. Similar service-oriented classes can be developed for network communication, printing devices, databases, etc.

We take this same approach when adding a user interface to our application. When we create user interface related classes, these classes should only contain logic related to capturing input from a user of our system, or displaying information to a user of our system. We usually "connect" our user interface classes to very few (often only one) classes in our domain layer.

This often requires changes to methods in the domain classes to provide information that the user interface classes need. In the simple UI depicted below, let's say that a user enters a UPC code into a text field and presses the "Scan" button, which causes product details to display.

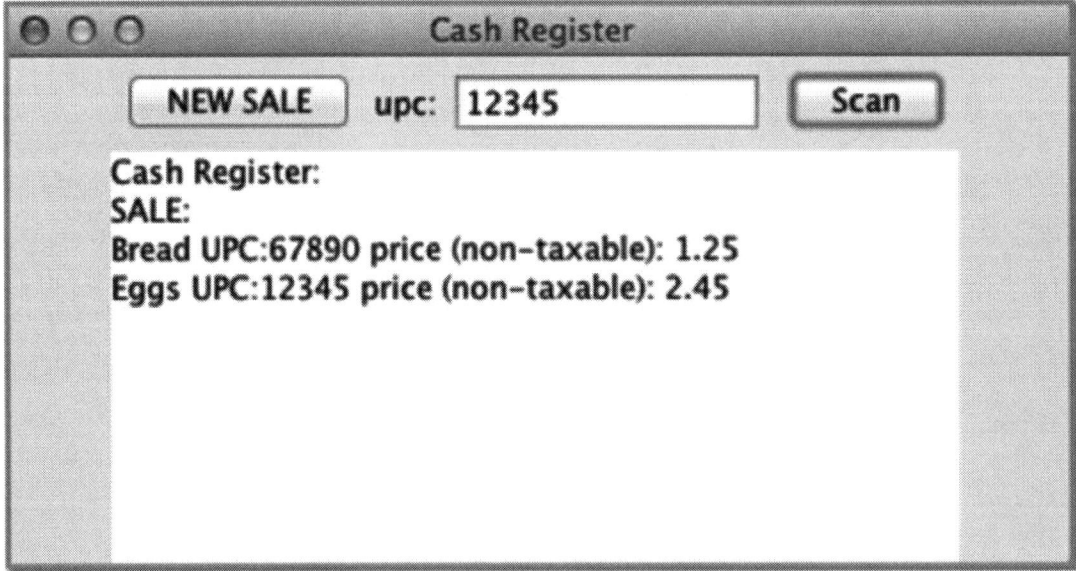

In this case, instead of putting a *println* statement in one of the *Product* class's methods that prints product details, a conversation will start between the CashRegister UI and the POSSystem domain class. POSSystem would ask its *Sale* to find the *Product* with that UPC Code, then *Sale* would retrieve the correct *Product* instance and it for its details. *Product's* method would return its description in a *String* to the *Sale* object, which would return that *String* to the *POSSystem* object, which would return that *String* to the UI object that started the whole conversation.

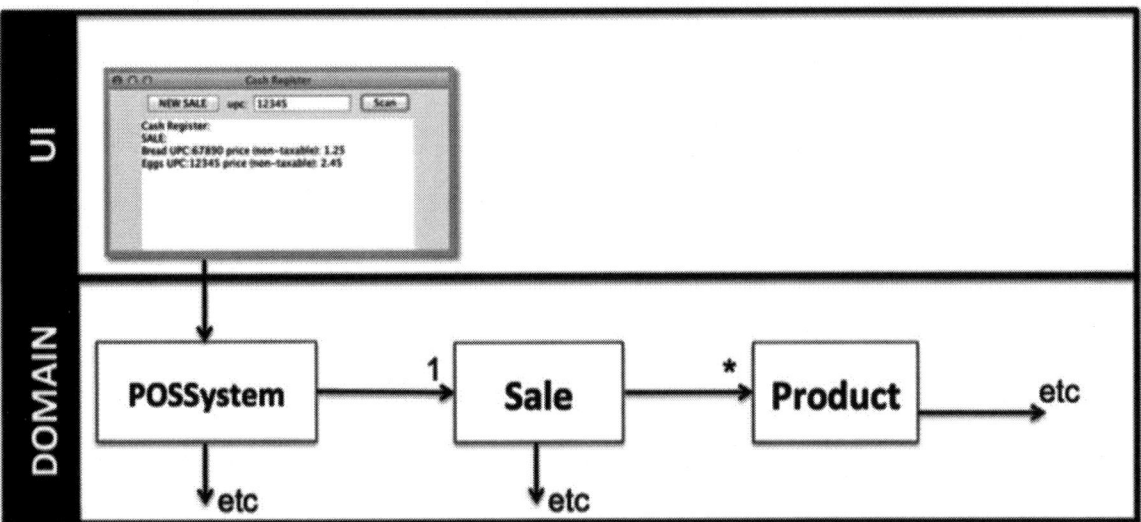

This may sound like a lot more trouble than putting *println* statements wherever we want them, but there's a reason we design systems this way. Let's say we build a sophisticated POS application that's works well with the user interface we developed on our Mac. What if we want to build an additional user interface to work with the same system? Nowadays, multiple user interfaces on the same system is the norm more so than the exception.

For example, I might want to connect my POSSystem to an actual cash register device, to a smart phone, a tablet, and a supermarket self checkout kiosk. We wouldn't want to duplicate all our POS logic in each of these implementations. Instead, we contain our POS logic to the domain classes, and connect each UI front-end to our POSSystem's starting class.

To enable such extensibility of our system, it's important to exclude all user interface related functionality from our domain layer. Also, we will want to create sufficient methods in our domain classes that handle requests for information that could come from one of multiple user interfaces.

Additionally, if we design our domain layer so all requests for information are serviced through a single class, it will be easier to connect new user interfaces to our system. This "starting" class brokers all requests for UI-related requests and passes them on to the domain classes that are best qualified to service them.

This layered approach to application architecture is how most computer systems are designed, and we will use this approach to learn user interface development with Java.

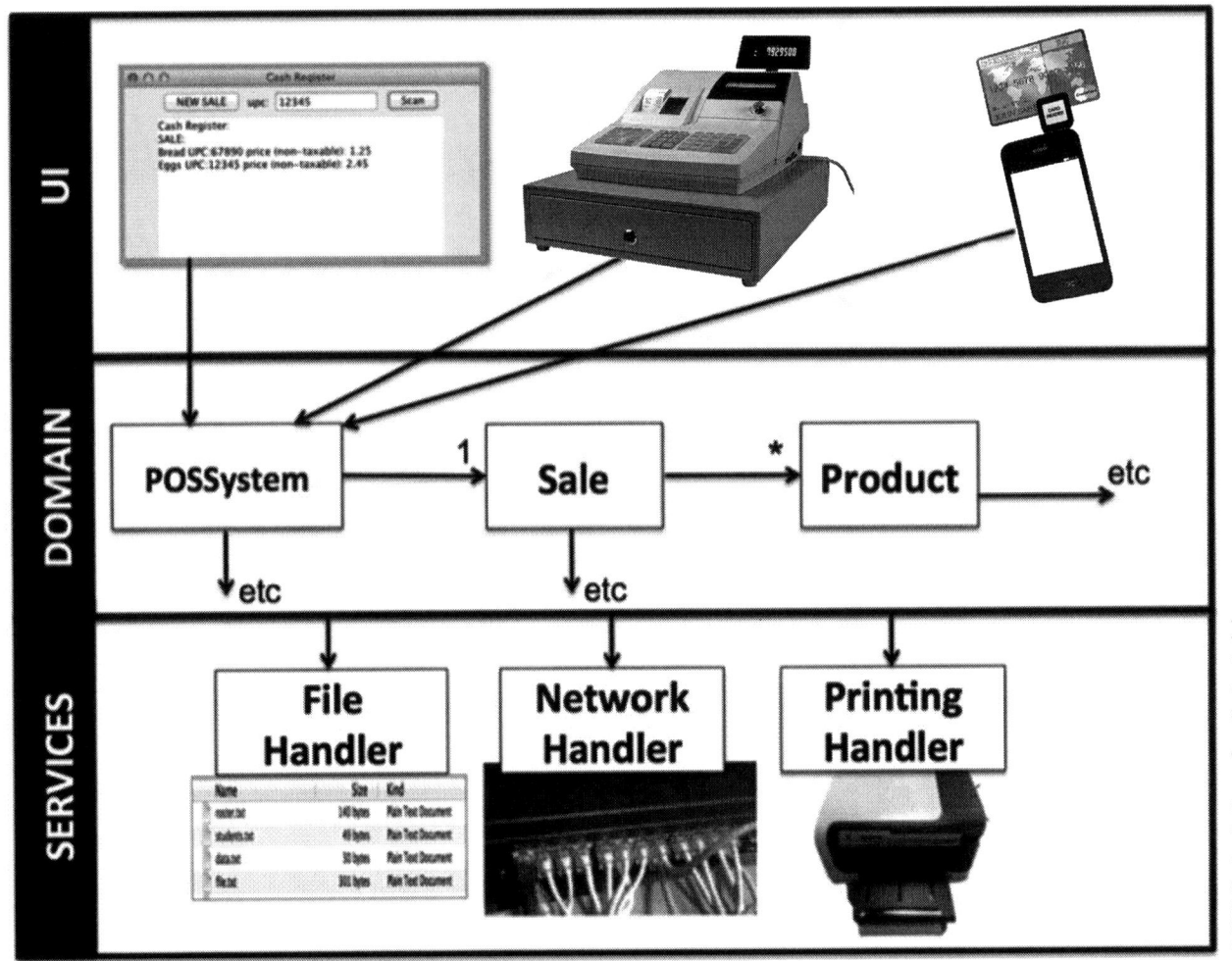

CREATING DATA INPUT DIALOGS

We will be introducing several new library classes to develop Java user interfaces. We'll start with something simple—a popup dialog. A modal dialog is a small window that halt execution of your program until the user responds to whatever it is asking for. Modal dialogs are usually used for displaying informational or warning messages, or for capturing a single piece of information.

The library class *javax.swing.JOptionPane* contains static methods that can be used to create quick dialogs on the fly. Since they are static methods, we don't need to create objects—we simply send messages to the *JOptionPane* class itself. Don't forget to import this class before using it:

```
import javax.swing.JOptionPane;
```

To capture a single *String* value from the user, we'll use *JOptionPane*'s *showInputDialog* method. This is very similar to using a *Scanner* object to capture a *String* from they user's keyboard input. The *showInputDialog* method has a *String* parameter, which will be displayed with an input field in the dialog:

```
JOptionPane.showInputDialog("Tell me your age");
```

This will result in the following dialog to pop up:

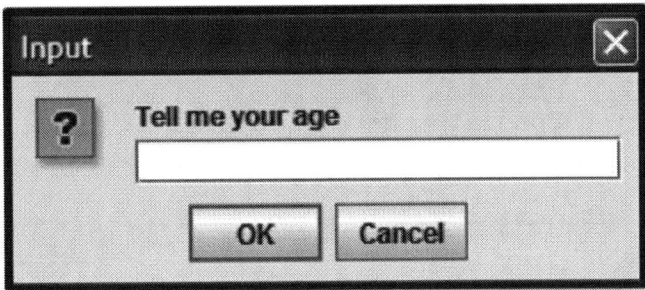

To test this, create a simple Tester class with a *main* method that invokes the dialog. To demonstrate the wait state that a dialog causes, try running the following program and pay attention to what displays on the console:

```java
import javax.swing.JOptionPane;
public class SampleGUI
{
    public static void main(String[] args)
    {
    System.out.println("Before dialog popup");
    JOptionPane.showInputDialog("Tell me your age");
    System.out.println("After dialog popup");
    }
}
```

When you run this, notice how the "After dialog popup" message doesn't appear until after you press the OK or Cancel button on the dialog and it disappears. With a dialog, your program will sit and wait at the line of code that creates the dialog until the user completes the requested action. When the action is completed, program execution resumes.

The *JOptionPane.showInputDialog* method returns a *String* that contains the contents of the field entered by the user. Note that it always returns a *String*, so if a number is needed, the *String* must be converted to a number. In this example, a way to convert the *String* to an int is to use the static method *parseInt* in the class *java. lang.Integer*. Since the library class *Integer* is in *java.lang*, it's not necessary to import it:

```java
//capture input from the dialog and save the result in aString
String aString = JOptionPane.showInputDialog("Tell me your age");

//convert aString to an int
int age = Integer.parseInt(aString);
```

This poses many possible problems at runtime, notably the user entering a non-integer value in the dialog. Regardless, for now we'll overlook the exception handling code that we would want to include.

CREATING MESSAGE DIALOGS

The library class *JOptionPane* has another static method that can be used to display a dialog with a message to the user. The *showMessageDialog* method has four parameters:

```java
JOptionPane.showMessageDialog(null, message, title, icon);
```

1st parameter: Specifies where on the screen to place the dialog, or null for placement at the center of the screen.

2nd parameter: A *String* containing the message to display.

3rd parameter: A *String* that will appear in the title bar of the dialog.

4th parameter: A static *JOptionPane* field that corresponds to these icons:

!	JOptionPane.ERROR _ MESSAGE
i	JOptionPane.INFORMATION _ MESSAGE
!	JOptionPane.WARNING _ MESSAGE
?	JOptionPane.QUESTION _ MESSAGE
(no icon)	JOptionPane.PLAIN _ MESSAGE

The following program will use *JOptionPane* methods to prompt the user for age, then it will display a message in another dialog:

```
import javax.swing.JOptionPane;
public class SampleGUI
{
  public static void main(String[] args) {
  //JOptionPane captures a single string:
  String s = JOptionPane.showInputDialog("Tell me your age");
  System.out.println("You are " + s + " years old.");
  //
  //Use static method parseInt in class Integer to convert String to int:
  //
  int age = Integer.parseInt(s);
  //What is the difference between the output of these two statements?
  System.out.println("Next year you will be " + age + 1 + " years old");
  System.out.println("Next year you will be " + (age + 1) + " years old");
  JOptionPane.showMessageDialog(
      null, //parameter 1: screen location
      "Next year you will be " + (age + 1) + " years old", //message
      "Age Output", //title
      JOptionPane.INFORMATION _ MESSAGE); //icon
  }
}
```

SWING AND AWT

We are going to learn how to use library classes in two Java GUI frameworks: Swing and Abstract Window-ing Toolkit (AWT). Basically, Swing classes are written 100% in Java and are portable as-is between different platforms. AWT classes, however, are linked to underlying windowing behavior in the host operating system. This makes AWT classes a bit "heavier-weight" than Swing classes, because they rely on the host operating system to take on some of its responsibilities. If you run an application on different operating systems, your Swing components will look identical on all platforms.

Regardless, we'll need a combination of Swing and AWT classes to build a complete working GUI in Java. Pay careful attention to which library each class you are introduced to resides in. All Swing and AWT classes must be imported before they can be used.

SWING

When starting with Swing, think of everything as either a container or a component. You create components and put them in containers. (Never mind the fact that a container is actually a component itself.)

Creating a GUI involves the following basic steps:

1. Create the container. We'll create a subclass of JFrame:

   ```
   public class MyFrame extends JFrame
   ```

2. Create a constructor in your JFrame subclass, and call the superclass constructor as its first step:

   ```
   public MyFrame() {
      super();
      //or super("tile"); to include a title in the JFrame's top border
   ```

3. Inside the constructor, create a layout manager to keep the frame's components organized. Send your *JFrame* the message *setLayout*, which is inherited from JFrame. *We'll* use *FlowLayout* for now:

   ```
   setLayout(new FlowLayout());
   ```

4. Create components (*JLabel, JButton, JList, etc.)* and add each to the container using the *add* method inherited from *JFrame*:

   ```
   JButton b = new JButton("Push"):
   add(b);

   add(new JLabel("a label"));
      }
   ```

That's all that's needed to create a basic JFrame with a couple components on it. For this to compile, you'll need to include import statements for all the library classes we used:

```
import javax.swing.JFrame;
import javax.swing.JLabel;
import javax.swting.JButton;
import java.awt.FlowLayout;
```

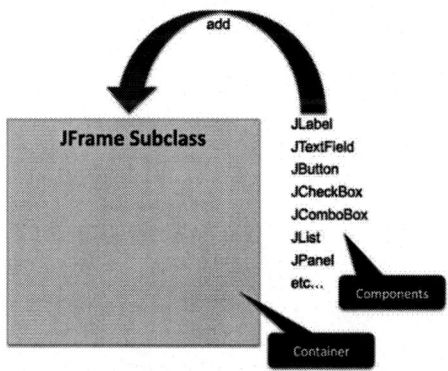

LAUNCHING A GUI

To run this program and try out our GUI, we'll create a *Tester* class with a *main* method that creates an instance of our *JFrame*. There are a couple messages we must send to our *JFrame* object for it to display and run properly. Also, don't forget to import *JFrame*:

```java
import javax.swing.JFrame;
public class GUITester
{
public static void main(String[] args)
{
   //Create an instance of your subclass of JFrame:
   FreewayUI f = new FreewayUI();

   //Tells the system what to do when the user closes the window
   //Without this, the window would disappear but still remain
   //in memory...this would be messy. The use of the static field
   //JFrame.EXIT _ ON _ CLOSE requires us to import JFrame above.
   f.setDefaultCloseOperation(JFrame.EXIT _ ON _ CLOSE);

   //Sets the width and height of the window in pixels
   f.setSize(400,200);

   //This is the line that makes the window appear
   f.setVisible(true);
}
}
```

LAYOUTS

Adding components to a *JFrame* container is just like throwing items into a barrel. You have no control over where the items will be located. To have better control over this, we create a *LayoutManager* object and connect it to our *JFrame*. The *LayoutManager* then takes on responsibility for managing the organization and placement of the components in the *JFrame*.

To demonstrate different *LayoutManager* objects, we'll create a simple *JFrame* with seven buttons:

```java
import javax.swing.JFrame;
import java.awt.FlowLayout;
import javax.swing.JButton;

public class LayoutTester extends JFrame
{
  public LayoutTester()
  {
  super("Layout Tester");
  FlowLayout fl = new FlowLayout();
  setLayout(fl);
  add(new JButton("One"));
  add(new JButton("Two"));
```

```
    add(new JButton("Three"));
    add(new JButton("Four"));
    add(new JButton("Five"));
    add(new JButton("Six"));
    add(new JButton("Seven"));
  }//end constructor
}//end class
```

The use of *FlowLayout*, causes all the buttons that fit to be placed across the first row, then across the second row, etc. The buttons on each row are centered on the *JFrame*. The height of the row is based on the height of the tallest component on the row. The result of running the application with a size of 400x200 is:

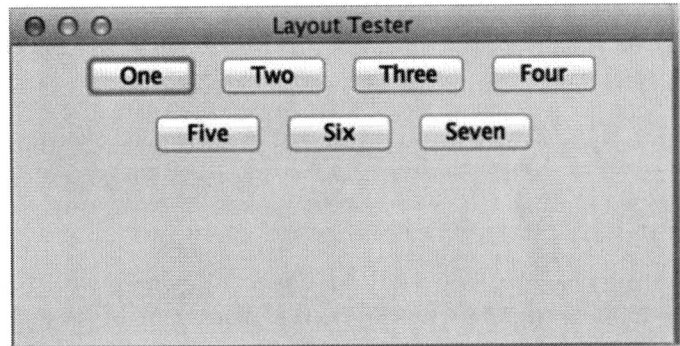

When the user shrinks or stretches the size of the window, the components will move based on the same layout strategy. This is managed by the *FlowLayout* object. If the window is shrunk to a size where the components don't fit, they will still be there, but won't be visible unless the user expands the size of the window:

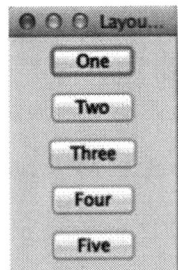 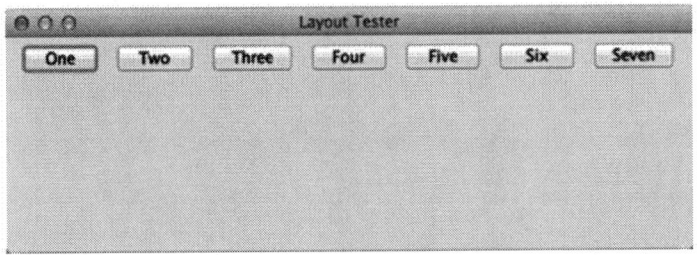 

Now let's use a different *LayoutManager* to see how it changes our *JFrame*. The *GridLayout* is constructed as a two-dimensional grid. You specify the number of rows and columns in *GridLayout*'s constructor. Each component you add to the *JFrame* will be placed inside one of the grid locations starting at the top, working left-to-right, top-to-bottom. Each component's size will be adjusted to maximize use of the grid cell it is contained in.

To demonstrate, first import the *GridLayout*:

```
    import java.awt.GridLayout;
```

Next, replace the *FlowLayout* with *GridLayout*, and include the grid dimensions:

```
    GridLayout gl = new GridLayout(3,3);
    setLayout(gl);
```

Without changing anything else in your program, notice how the buttons are automatically resized to fill each grid cell location:

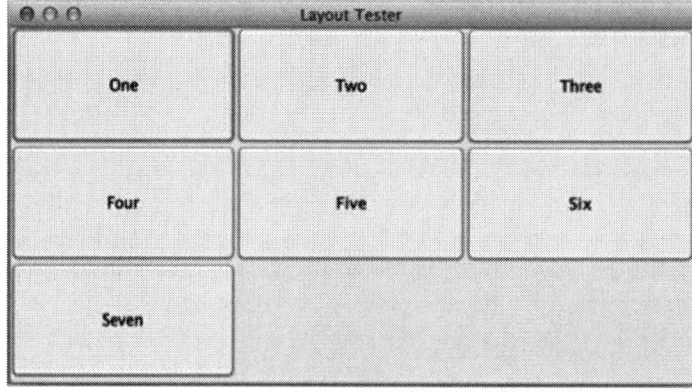

When the user shrinks or expands the size of a *JFrame* that uses *GridLayout*, the components in the *JFrame* will shrink or grow with the window, retaining their location on the grid.

There are several other *LayoutManager* classes, but as beginners we can stick with these two.

JCOMPONENT

The steepest part of the learning curve of new GUI developers is learning which components exist, and are best suited to different types of user interface needs. We'll explore some of these, but this is not intended to be a comprehensive inventory of all swing *JComponent* objects.

The program below includes a sampling of commonly used components. Note all the import statements. You could use a wildcard and import javax.swing.*, but that would import unnecessary classes, which consumes resources you don't need.

Read the comments in the sample program to learn how to handle each of the *JComponent* types. Note that the JList is shown twice – with and without a JScrollPane. Also note how the JRadioButton objects are bound together as a ButtonGroup so turning one on will turn off the others.

```java
import javax.swing.JFrame;
import java.awt.FlowLayout;
import javax.swing.JButton;
import javax.swing.JCheckBox;
import javax.swing.JLabel;
import javax.swing.JTextField;
import javax.swing.JPasswordField;
import javax.swing.JList;
import javax.swing.JScrollPane;
import javax.swing.JRadioButton;
import javax.swing.ButtonGroup;
import javax.swing.JTextArea;

public class LayoutTester extends JFrame
{

public LayoutTester()
{
super("Layout Tester");
//Create and set FlowLayout
FlowLayout fl = new FlowLayout();
setLayout(fl);
```

```
//Create and add two JButtons
JButton jb = new JButton("Please Press me!!!");
add(jb);
add(new JButton("No please press me!!"));

//Create and add a label and text input field of size 20
add(new JLabel("Name"));
add(new JTextField(20));

//Create and add a JCheckBox with its label
JCheckBox jcb = new JCheckBox("Check this");
add(jcb);
//Create four JRadioButton instances:
JRadioButton jrb1 = new JRadioButton("Dog");
JRadioButton jrb2 = new JRadioButton("Cat");
JRadioButton jrb3 = new JRadioButton("Other");
//add them to the JFrame
add(jrb1);
add(jrb2);
add(jrb3);

//Bind together the three JRadioButtons so turning on one
//turns off the others:
ButtonGroup bg = new ButtonGroup();
bg.add(jrb1);
bg.add(jrb2);
bg.add(jrb3);

//Create a standard JList without scroll bars.
//Pass it an array of strings to populate the list:
String[] colors = {"Red", "Green", "Blue","Yellow","Black","Brown","White",
"Purple","Maroon"};
add(new JList(colors));

//Create another JList, but also create a JScrollPane and pass it the
JList:
JList jl = new JList(colors);
JScrollPane jsp = new JScrollPane(jl, JScrollPane.VERTICAL _ SCROLLBAR _
ALWAYS, JScrollPane.HORIZONTAL _ SCROLLBAR _ NEVER);
add(jsp);

//Create and add a label and a password field, which doesn't display the
text that is entered
add(new JLabel("password:"));
add(new JPasswordField(10));

//Create a JTextArea of 10 rows by 25 columns
//then create another JScrollPane and add the JTextArea to it
//Set both scrollbars to "ALWAYS"
//Finally, add the JScrollPane to the JFrame
JTextArea jta = new JTextArea(10,25);
```

```
JScrollPane jsp2 = new JScrollPane(jta, JScrollPane.VERTICAL _ SCROLL-
BAR _ ALWAYS, JScrollPane.HORIZONTAL _ SCROLLBAR _ ALWAYS);
add(jsp2);
}//end constuctor

    }//end class
```

The resulting JFrame should look like this. You may want to adjust the dimensions of your JFrame in the *main* method that creates it. The FlowLayout may frustrate you as components shift location based on the width of the window.

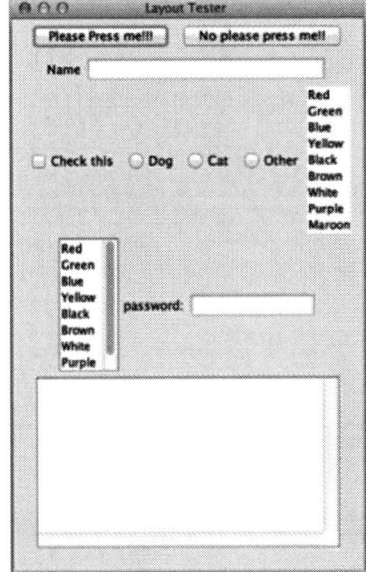

GUI PAINTERS

Selecting GUI components and laying them out can be very tedious using this manual approach. Professional programmers would most likely use a GUI building tool to lay out the contents of the *JFrame* as well as to select the best *LayoutManager* to associate with it.

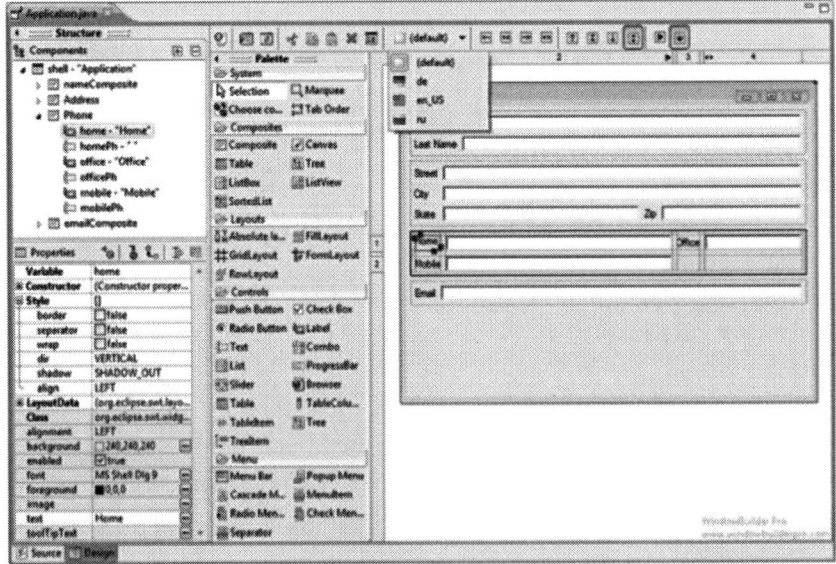

Eclipse offers a tool called *WindowBuilder* (shown above) that allows you to design your GUI, then it generates all the Java code for you. While this is much more efficient and fool proof, it's not recommended for introductory students. The best way to understand the underlying GUI code is to build it from scratch for a while.

\\INTERFACES

The sample *JFrames* we have built so far have all sorts of interesting things on them, but they don't really do anything. When you click the button, it reacts to the press, but it doesn't make anything happen. Next we'll learn how to add behavior to those components that trigger a response.

Before we can do that, we need to learn about another element of the Java language that we haven't used yet: *Interfaces*. *Interfaces* are not a part of Java's *swing* or *awt* frameworks, but they are required to implement behavior in a GUI.

An interface looks like a class, but it actually contains no data, and its methods contain no logic. An interface exists strictly to enforce the implementation of classes that are associated with it.

For example, we could create the following interface to enforce the implementation of certain methods:

```
public interface Animalistic
{
  void speak();
  int getAge();
  void setBreed(String s);
}
```

This would be compiled just like a *class*, and the compiler would create a file with a *.class* extension that looks like a class. Note that interface methods only have method signatures with a terminator; none of the *interface's* methods have a method body.

By itself, an interface is of no value. Its use comes into play by connecting it with a class using the keyword *implements*. Let's create a class named *Lion* and we want to force it to have the three methods that are defined in the *interface* Animalistic. By declaring that the *Lion* class *implements Animalistic*, the Java compiler will require the class *Lion* to contain those three methods. It doesn't matter what the contents are, but the methods must exist in *Lion*:

```
public class Lion implements Animalistic
{
public void speak()
{//do something }

public int getAge()
{return 0;}

public void setBreed(String s)
{//do something}

}
```

Why bother with interfaces? Certain frameworks require them. When a programmer develops a class that needs to work within an established framework, components of the framework may need to send certain messages to the new class. By requiring that the class implements a certain interface, the framework components can be assured that the new class has methods to respond to those messages.

As part of the Java GUI framework, we will be creating classes must implement one of the GUI framework's interfaces. This will force you to include methods that are part of that interface.

We'll come back to interfaces later. Now we need to look at another Java language element that is needed to use the GUI framework: Inner classes.

INNER CLASSES

When we started to learn object oriented programming, we learned that we could create and send messages to instances of other classes, as long as we had direct access to them. Access was managed by putting all the classes in the same package.

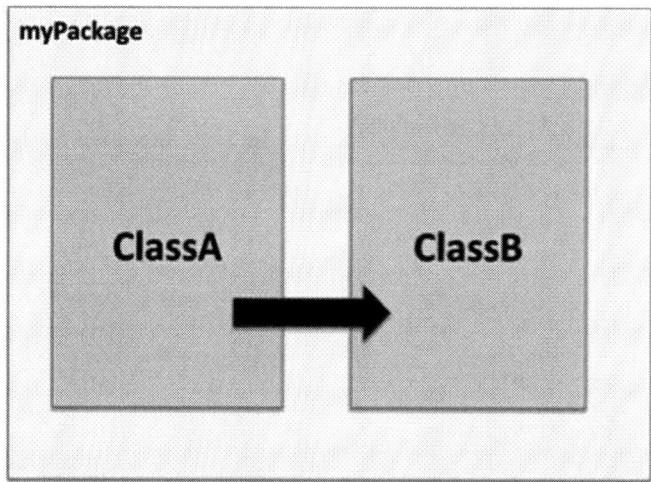

We also learned that we could create and send messages to other classes from different packages, as long as we imported those classes.

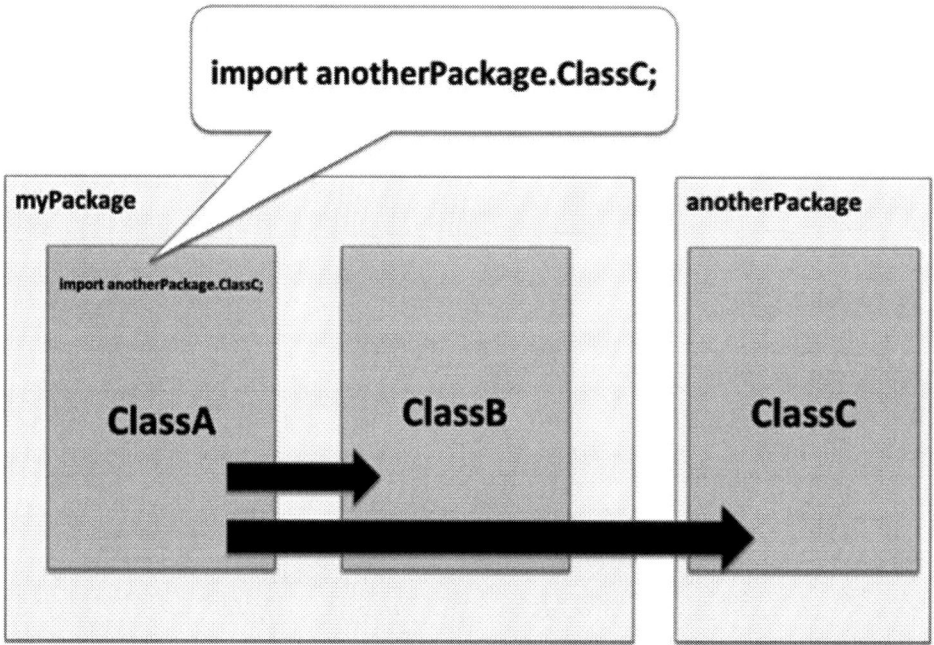

Next, we're going in the opposite direction. Instead of expanding our visibility to classes inside our same package, or in some other package, let's look at creating a much narrower scope for visibility to a class—inside a class. A class defined inside another class. This is referred to as an inner class.

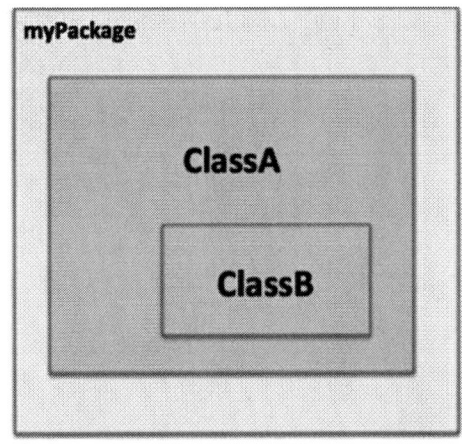

With an inner class, *ClassB* is defined completely inside the contents (curly braces) of *ClassA*.

This narrows access to *ClassB*—instances of *ClassB* can only be created and communicated with within an instance of *ClassA*.

Let's look at an example of this in Java. In the first example, we have two independent classes: *Auto* and *Wheel*.

Auto and *Wheel* are both public classes, and *Auto* has an array containing instances of class *Wheel*. Since *Wheel* is public, other classes could also associate to instances of the same *Wheel* class that *Auto* is associated with.

```java
public class Auto {
   private Wheel[] wheels = new Wheel[4];
   public Auto()
        {
        wheels[0]  = new Wheel("LeftFront");
        wheels[1]  = new Wheel("RightFront");
        wheels[2]  = new Wheel("LeftRear");
        wheels[3]  = new Wheel("RightRear");
        }
}
```

```java
public class Wheel {
   private String name;

   public Wheel(String s)
   {
   name = s;
   }
}
```

In this second example, we'll make *Wheel* an inner class of *Auto*:

```java
public class Auto {
private Wheel[] wheels = new Wheel[4];
public Auto()
   {
   wheels[0]  = new Wheel("LeftFront");
   wheels[1]  = new Wheel("RightFront");
   wheels[2]  = new Wheel("LeftRear");
   wheels[3]  = new Wheel("RightRear");
   }
```

```
private class Wheel {
    private String name;
    public Wheel(String s)
    {
    name = s;
    }

}
}
```

Note that the code is almost identical in both examples with two exceptions:

- In the second example, class *Wheel* is declared as *private*
- In the second example, the entire contents of class *Wheel* are contained within the curly braces of class *Auto*.

The use of inner classes is very restricting—in this example, class *Wheel* can only ever be used by instances of class *Auto*. The *Wheel* class cannot be reused by other components.

Why would we do this, since it restricts the reusability of the inner class? We'll explain as we continue to learn Java's GUI framework. Inner classes are an integral part of that framework. For now, though, just make sure you understand the construct of inner classes.

THE JAVA ACTIONLISTENER INTERFACE

We had previously created a *JFrame* container and we added some *JComponent*s to it. Some of these components have no possible behavior associated with them (such as *JLabels*.) Other *JComponents* such as *JButtons* are going to be pressed eventually, and we're going to need to do something about it.

Handling behavior in a Java GUI is not complex, but it's also non-trivial. We must do the following:

1. Create an inner class within our *JFrame* that will handle all functions that *JComponent*'s need done. When declaring the method signature of the inner class, it should implement the interface **java.awt. event.ActionListener**. (import this interface!)

    ```
    import java.awt.event.ActionListener;

    public class LayoutTester extends JFrame {

            //All the stuff you created previously

            private class MyInnerClass implements ActionListener
            {
    ```

2. Because the *ActionListener* interface requires a method with the signature *actionPerformed(ActionEvent e)*, create this (and only this) method inside the inner class inside your *JFrame* class.
    ```
    public void actionPerformed(ActionEvent e)
    {
    //do stuff (see step 4)
    }
    ```

3. Associate each *JComponent* that you plan to respond to with an instance of your inner class.

```
//back in the JFrame constructor
//Create and add two JButtons
JButton jb = new JButton("Please Press me!!!");
add(jb);
MyInnerClass mic = new MyInnerClass(); //Create an instance of the inner
                                       //class you created


jb.addActionListener(mic);            //Link JButton jb to that inner
                                      //class instance
```

4. Create logic to handle behavior for each of your *JComponent's* that may be clicked, pressed, or otherwise triggered inside the *actionPeformed* method that you previously created.

```
//inside the inner class MyInnerClass
//add logic to its required (due to the interface method actionPerformed:
//that does what it needs to do when the button is pressed:

//replace "doStuff" in step 2 above with:
System.out.println("Button was pressed"); /or something more interesting
```

Let's look at a complete example now:

```
import javax.swing.JFrame;
import java.awt.FlowLayout;
import javax.swing.JButton;
import java.awt.event.ActionListener;
import java.awt.event.ActionEvent;
public class MyUI extends JFrame
{
  public MyUI()
  {
  super();
  setLayout(new FlowLayout());
  JButton b1 = new JButton("Push me");
  add(b1);
  MyInner mi = new MyInner();
  b1.addActionListener(mi);
  } //end constructor

  private class MyInner implements ActionListener {
        public void actionPerformed(ActionEvent e)
        {
        System.out.println("Pushed button");
        }//end method actionPerformed
  }//end inner class MyInner
}//end class MyUI
```

Now let's look closer at what each part of that program does:

```java
import javax.swing.JFrame;
import java.awt.FlowLayout;
import javax.swing.JButton;
import java.awt.event.ActionListener;
import java.awt.event.ActionEvent;

public class MyUI extends JFrame
{
    public MyUI()
    {
        super();
        setLayout(new FlowLayout());
        JButton b1 = new JButton("Push me");
        add(b1);
        MyInner mi = new MyInner();
        b1.addActionListener(mi);
    } //end constructor

    private class MyInner implements ActionListener {
        public void actionPerformed(ActionEvent e)
        {
        System.out.println("Pushed button");
        }//end method actionPerformed
    }//end inner class MyInner
}//end class MyUI
```

Push me

- Create the JButton
- Add it to the JFrame
- Create a MyInner instance
- Associate it to the JButton
- Invoked whenever the Jbutton is pressed

CHANGING WINDOW CONTENTS AT RUNTIME

Let's shift away from using the console to test our GUI. Instead, let's add a text field that gets changed when the button is pressed. This will expose the need to make a minor change to the way we have organized our program.

Let's add a blank *JLabel* to our *JFrame* by adding these three lines of code:

```
//Above our class signature:
import javax.swing.JLabel;

//Insert below the lines that create and add the JButton.
//This will create an empty JLabel and add it to the JFrame:
JLabel label = new JLabel();
add(label);
```

Next we want to display some text in the *JLabel* when the button is pressed. Since the button press causes the *actionPerformed* method to be executed, the code to change the *JLabel* contents would need to be inside the *actionPerformed* method.

To change the contents of a *JLabel*, send it the *setText* message with a *String*:

```
label.setText("Thank you!");
```

If you try putting that inside the *actionPerformed* method, however, it won't compile. The problem is lack of visibility to the variable *label*. The JLabel was declared inside the *MyUI* constructor, so the variable *label* can only be used inside the constructor.

To resolve this, move the declaration of the variable *label* outside the constructor, but still inside the class *MyUI*. This will make that variable accessible by any method inside *MyUI*, including methods belonging to its inner classes. By the way, this is the reason Java's GUI framework uses inner classes.

TIP: Always declare the variables for your *JComponents* outside the constructor so they can be accessed in the inner class's *actionPerformed* method.

After moving the declarations outside the constructor, our program should now look like this, and when you press the button, the label contents should appear:

```java
import javax.swing.JFrame;
import java.awt.FlowLayout;
import javax.swing.JButton;
import java.awt.event.ActionListener;
import java.awt.event.ActionEvent;
import javax.swing.JLabel;

public class MyUI extends JFrame {
JLabel label;
JButton b1;

    public MyUI() {
    super();
    setLayout(new FlowLayout());
    b1 = new JButton("Push me");
    add(b1);

    label = new JLabel();
    add(tf);

    MyInner mi = new MyInner();
    b1.addActionListener(mi);
    } //end constructor

    private class MyInner implements ActionListener {

        public void actionPerformed(ActionEvent e)
        {
        label.setText("Thank you!");
        }//end method actionPerformed
    }//end inner class MyInner
}//end class MyUI
```

HANDLING MULTIPLE ACTIONS

What if there was more than one *JButton* on the *JFrame*? One approach would be to create a second inner class, whose *actionPerformed* method contains the logic to respond to the second button being pressed. Try it:

Declare another *JButton* outside the constructor:

```java
JButton b2;
```

Create the second *JButton* inside the constructor and add it to the *JFrame*:

```
b2 = new JButton("PANIC!");
add(b2);
```

Create another inner class that changes the contents of the *JLabel*:

```
private class MySecondInner implements ActionListener {
   public void actionPerformed(ActionEvent e)
   {
   label.setText("Yikes!!");
   }//end method actionPerformed
}//end inner class MySecondInner
```

Finally, go back to the constructor and associate the new *JButton* to an instance of the new inner class:

```
b2.addActionListener(new MySecondInner());
```

Now when you run your program, the *JLabel* contents will change back and forth as you press each of the buttons.

This approach can work for a couple *JButtons*, but what if you have several buttons, and a menu with several menu options, and other types of *JComponent* that trigger a response? It would be messy to create an inner class for every *JComponent* on our *JFrame* that triggers behavior.

Java does provide a way of creating quick unnamed (anonymous) inner classes on the fly, but we'll defer that as an advanced topic. Instead, let's learn how to function with a single inner class that supports multiple *JComponent* objects.

Note the parameter of the *actionPerformed* method "*ActionEvent e.*" The variable *e* contains a reference to the *JComponent* that triggered the action. If you send *e* the message *getSource()*, it will return a reference to the *JComponent* that was pressed, clicked, touched, etc., and caused the *actionPerformed* method to be invoked.

By getting the result of *e.getSource()* and comparing it to our components *b1* and *b2*, we'll know which button was pressed. Let's delete the second inner class and modify our original inner class to support both buttons:

```
private class MyInner implements ActionListener {
   public void actionPerformed(ActionEvent e) {
   if(e.getSource() == b1)
      label.setText("Thank you!");
   if(e.getSource() == b2)
      label.setText("Yikes!!");
   }//end method actionPerformed
}//end inner class MyInner
```

Now go back to your constructor and associate *JButton* b2 with the same inner class instance that *JButton* b1 is associated with:

```
b2.addActionListener(mi);
```

This version of the program should function the same way as the version with two inner classes, but the code is cleaner. As you add more components with behavior, just associate each of them to your inner class and add an additional *if* statement in its *actionPerformed* method.

CONNECTING THE GUI TO THE DOMAIN

Back at the beginning of the chapter, we described a layered architecture. Now that we know how to create a user interface in Java, let's learn how to connect it to our domain classes. We'll also use this as an opportunity to walk through a complete GUI example step-by-step.

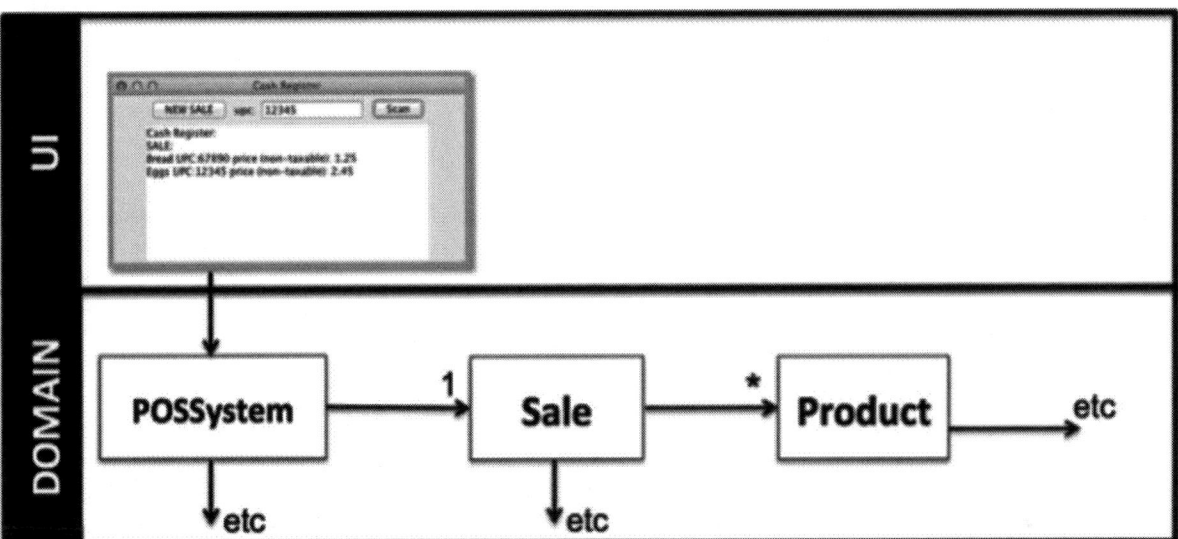

For starters, create the JFrame subclass and start the constructor with a call to the superclass constructor, and set the layout to a FlowLayout instance:

```
import javax.swing.JFrame;
import java.awt.FlowLayout;

public class POSWindow extends JFrame
{
public POSWindow()
{
  super("Cash Register");
  setLayout(new FlowLayout());
}//end constructor
}//end class
```

Declare variables for a JButton, JLabel, JTextField, another JButton, and a JTextArea. Also import the classes for each of these. Don't forget to add the components to the frame:

```
import javax.swing.JFrame;
import java.awt.FlowLayout;
```

```
import javax.swing.JButton;
import javax.swing.JLabel;
import javax.swing.JTextField;
import javax.swing.JTextArea;
```

```
public class POSWindow extends JFrame
{
```

```
private JButton newSaleButton;
private JLabel upcLabel;
private JTextField upcField;
private JButton scanButton;
private JTextArea textArea;
```

```
public POSWindow()
{
super("Cash Register");
setLayout(new FlowLayout());
```

```
newSaleButton = new JButton("NEW SALE");
upcLabel = new JLabel("upc code");
upcField = new JTextField(10);
scanButton = new JButton("Scan");
textArea = new JTextArea(10,20);
add(newSaleButton);
add(upcLabel);
add(upcField);
add(scanButton);
add(textArea);
```

```
}//end constructor
}//end class
```

Let's test what we have so far. We'll need another class with a *main* method to create and launch the *POSWindow* instance. Let's call it *POSLauncher*. You may have to experiment a bit with the frame dimensions so the components wrap properly. A different layout manager would make this easier, but would also require a lot more knowledge of a different layout type (e.g., GridBagLayout.) For now, we'll continue to muddle along with *FlowLayout*:

```
import javax.swing.JFrame;

public class POSLauncher
{
public static void main(String[] args) {
POSWindow pw = new POSWindow();
pw.setDefaultCloseOperation(JFrame.EXIT _ ON _ CLOSE);
pw.setSize(500,300);
pw.setVisible(true);
}}
```

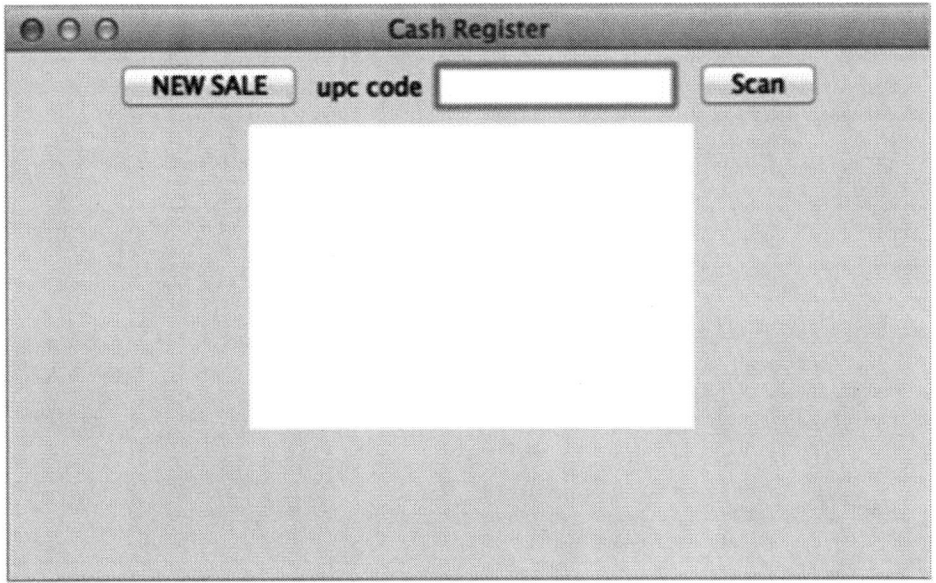

Now let's get back to our *POSWindow* and add behavior so the window behaves like a cash register. The model below depicts our *POSLauncher* and our *POSWindow* along with a link to the domain class *POSSystem*.

Let's assume the *POSSystem* class exists and has method *scan*, which uses the *int* parameter passed to it to find a *Product* instance and adds it to its *Sale* instance.

For the purposes of learning how to build the GUI, we won't expose the details of the domain classes. Just assume that the *POSSystem* domain class knows how to scan an item. It also can return a text representation of the details of its *Sale* via the method *getSaleDetails*, which we will use to populate our *JTextArea*. Finally, the POSSystem has a method named *newSale*, which will create a new *Sale* object when invoked.

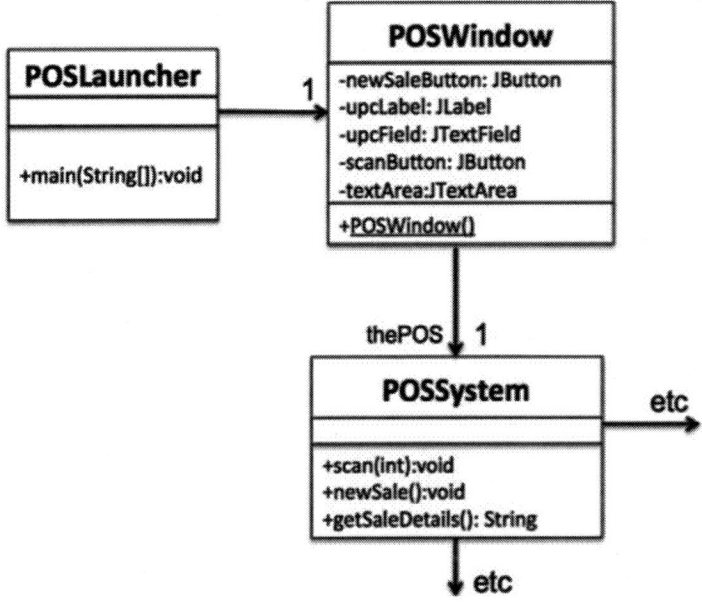

To add behavior to our *POSWindow*, we'll need to start by creating an instance of *POSSystem* when we start up our *POSWindow*. Based on the model, we'll name it *thePOS*. By declaring and creating *thePOS* at the top of the *POSWindow* class definition, we'll be able to send it messages from within the constructor or in the inner class:

```
public class POSWindow extends JFrame
{
private POSSystem thePOS = new POSSystem;
private JButton newSaleButton;
private JLabel upcLabel;
private JTextField upcField;
private JButton scanButton;
private JTextArea textArea;
...
```

Next, let's create an inner class that implements the interface *ActionListener*. Don't forget to import *ActionListener* and *ActionEvent*. Let's program our *actionPerformed* method to respond to the following actions:

1. When the *newSaleButton* is pressed, send a *newSale()* message to *thePOS*.
2. When the *scanButton* is pressed, get the contents of *upcField*, convert it to an *int* and send it a parameter to *thePOS*'s method *scan(int)*.
3. After either button is pressed, also send the *getSaleDetails()* message to *thePOS* and update the contents of *textArea*.

Let's get started. First, add these import statements:

```
import java.awt.event.ActionListener;
import java.awt.event.ActionEvent;
```

omitted details

Next, create the inner class and add the behavior described above to the *actionPerformed* method:

```
//Insert this in the POSWindow class after the closing curly brace of
// the constructor but before the closing curly brace of the class

private class MyInner implements ActionListener {
public void actionPerformed(ActionEvent e) {

  if(e.getSource() == newSaleButton)
       thePOS.newSale();

  if(e.getSource() == scanButton) {
       int x = Integer.parseInt(upcField.getText());
       thePOS.scan(x);
       }

  String s = thePOS.getSaleDetails();
  textArea.setText(s);

}//end method actionPerformed
```

Finally, go back to the constructor and put logic that creates an instance of the *MyInner* inner class and associates both buttons to it:

```
MyInner mi = new MyInner();
newSaleButton.addActionListener(mi);
scanButton.addActionListener(mi);
```

Without a *POSSystem* class, you won't be able to test this. For testing purposes, you could create what's referred to as a "stub" – a partial program that has just enough code to compile and provide an interface that your window can send messages to. Here is an example:

```
public class POSSystem {
  public void scan(int x) { }

  public void newSale() {}

  public String getSaleDetails()
  { return "Bogus sale"; }
}
```

A p p e n d i x   A
JDK INSTALLATION

These instructions install the Java Development Kit (JDK) on your computer may vary a bit from what's needed due to frequent changes to operating system versions and versions of the JDK.

Mac computers used to ship with the JDK already installed. Newer Mac operating systems no longer ship with the JDK, but if you try to execute a Java command, the Mac will automatically download and install the JDK on your machine.

Windows computers rarely ship with the JDK installed, so you will most likely need to follow the installation instructions in this appendix.

First, follow the steps in this flowchart to determine whether or not the JDK is already installed on your computer:

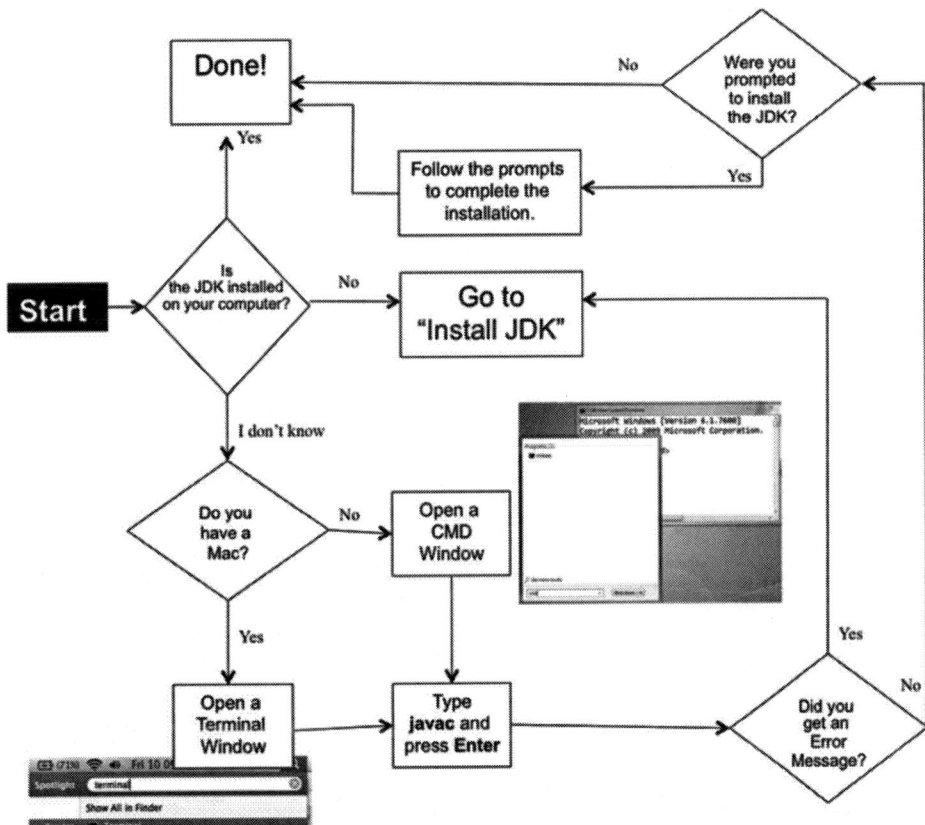

If the JDK is present on your computer, stop, you're done. If not, continue the steps in the flowchart below:

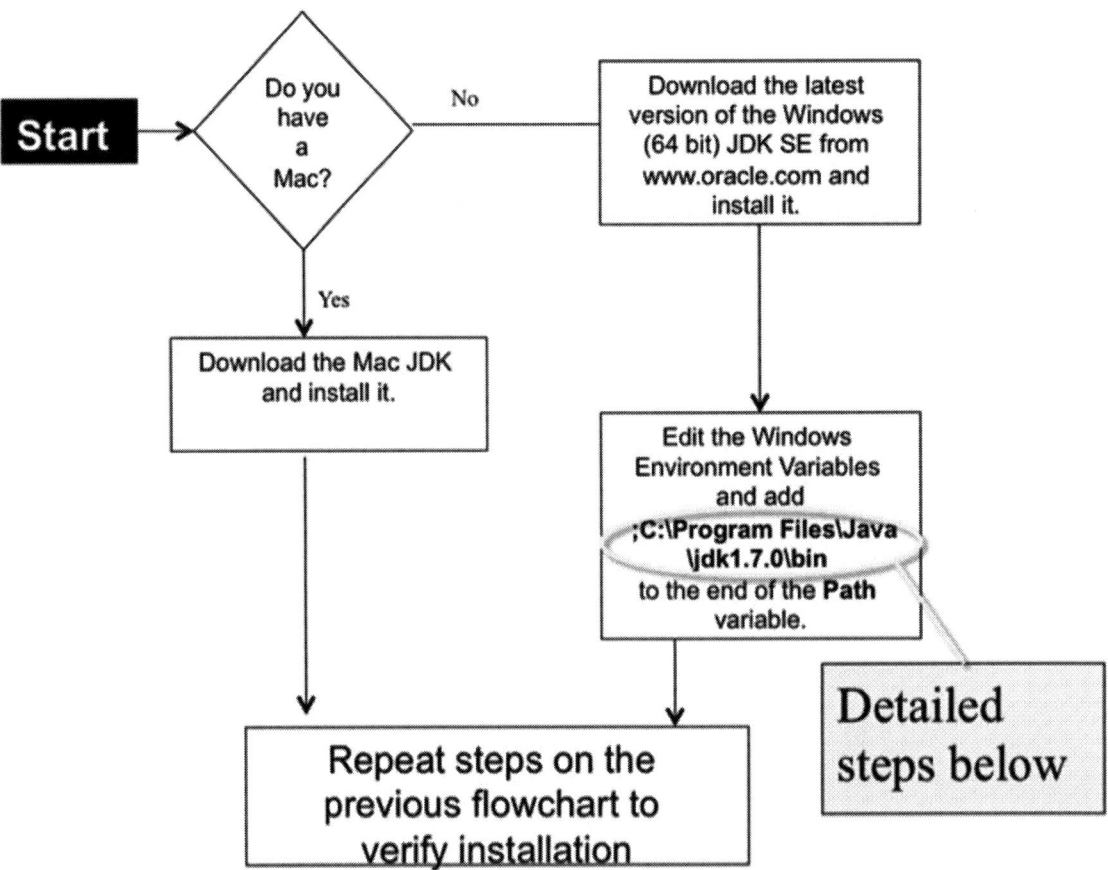

Windows users: Change your PATH environment variable so you can run the Java compiler and JVM from any folder on your system:

Open Windows Explorer and look at C:\Program Files\Java for the correct path name to include here. The subdirectory name will match whatever version of Java you downloaded.

For jdk1.7.0, the following text should be appended at the end of the PATH environment variable. Don't forgot the semicolon in front:

```
;C:\Program Files\Java\jdk1.7.0\bin
```

See screen shots of the Windows 7 environment variable dialog on the next page.

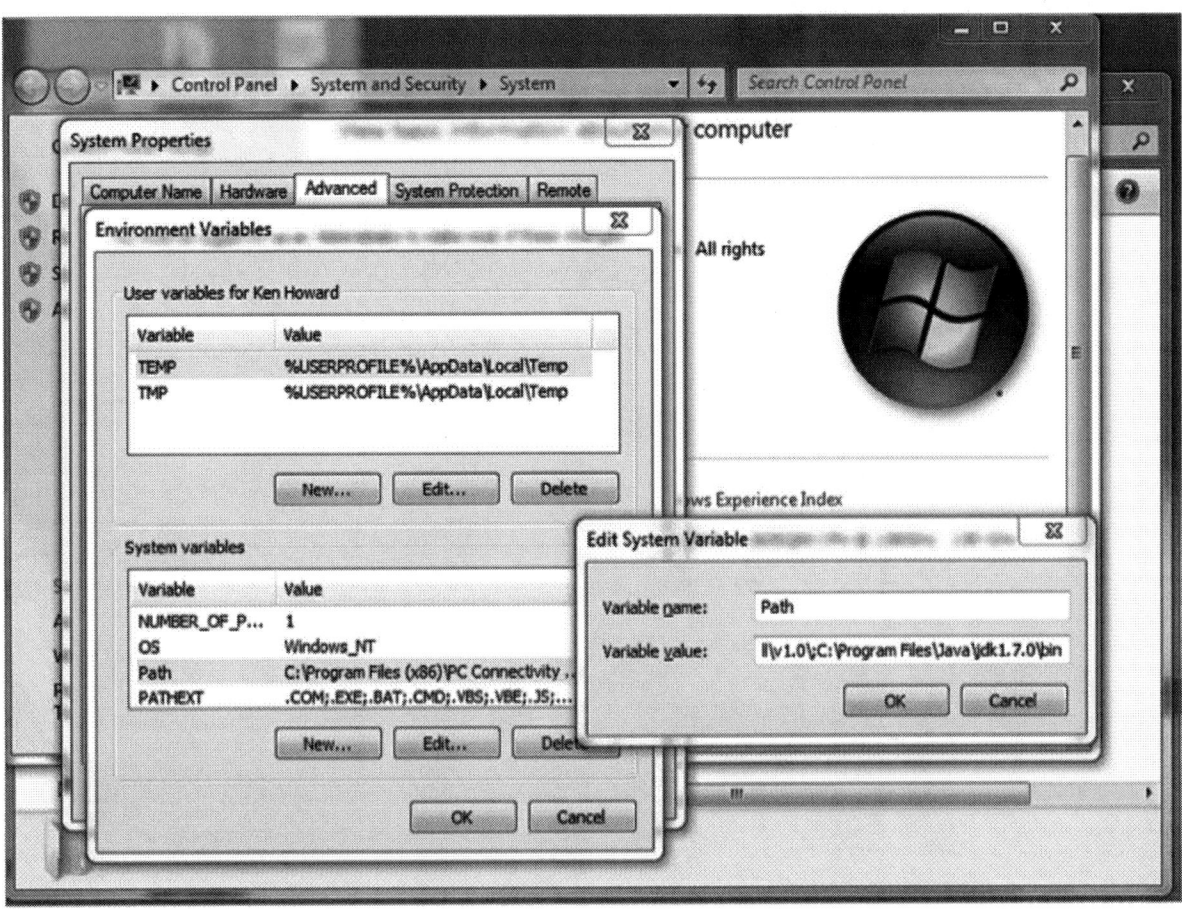

MAC/WINDOWS COMMANDS

The following table lists the most common terminal/cmd commands that you'll need to navigate folders and find files to compile and run:

WINDOWS	MAC	ACTION
DIR	ls	List directory contents
CD *dirName*	cd *dirName*	Move down the directory the directory named *dir*Name the next level down
CD ..	cd ..	Move up one directory in the directory hierarchy
CD \	CD /	Move up to the root directory
MKDIR MD *dirName*	mkdir *dirName*	Make a new directory named *dirName*
RMDIR RD *dirName*	rmdir	Remove a directory
CHDIR	pwd	Display directory location
DEL *fileName* ERASE *fileName*	rm *fileName*	Remove the file named *fileName*
COPY *file1 file2*	cp *file1 file2*	Copy a file named *file1* to a new file named *file2*
RENAME *file1 newname*	mv *file1 newname*	Rename a file
TYPE *filename*	cat *filename*	Display contents of *filename* to user's screen
MORE *filename*	more *filename*	Type (or cat) contents of *filename* one screen of text at a time
CLS	clear	Clear screen
EXIT	exit	Exit the terminal or cmd window

APPENDIX C
HEX/BINARY/DECIMAL NUMBERS

Three number systems are important to Computer Science, and it's helpful to know how to interpret values represented in each of these systems.

BASE 10

Base 10 is the most readily understood numeric system in our culture. It's the system we learned in grade school, and that we use in most of our everyday life. In base 10 (or decimal), ten values (digits) are used to represent each "position" in a number. Those values are 0, 1, 2, 3, 4, 5, 6, 7, 8, and 9. For integer (non floating point) values, each position in a number is read from the right to the left:

etc...	0..9	0..9	0..9	0..9	0..9	0..9
	100,000's	10,000's	1,000's	100's	10's	1's

Therefore, the number 2345 is equivalent to the value (working from right to left):

```
(5 * 1) + (4 * 10) + (3 * 100) + (2 * 1000)
```

You were likely taught this fundamental math function in grade school. Reviewing how to break a base 10 number down into its component parts will help you better learn/understand other numbering systems.

BASE 2

In the base 2 numbering system, there are only two digits in each position: 0 or 1. These values area also referred to as *binary numbers*. Binary values are important in computer science because communication with and from computers occurs via pulses of electronic signals.

A sequence of either the presence (1) or absence (0) of a pulse form a code that can be translated to human consumable information. Each pulse (or absence of pulse) is referred to as a *bit*, and eight of these in a row form what's referred to as a *byte*.

Each *byte* can be mapped to a human consumable thing such as a letter of the alphabet. One translation table called ASCII ("Askey") was selected the U.S. national standard for mapping bytes to characters. The

ASCII table represents each character as a binary number, decimal number, and hexadecimal number. As an example, the ASCII translation of the binary number 01001010 is the capital letter J:

CHARACTER	BINARY	DECIMAL	HEXADECIMAL
J	01001010	74	4A

The following illustration shows the series of pulses that is chunked into four bytes that map to the letters Java:

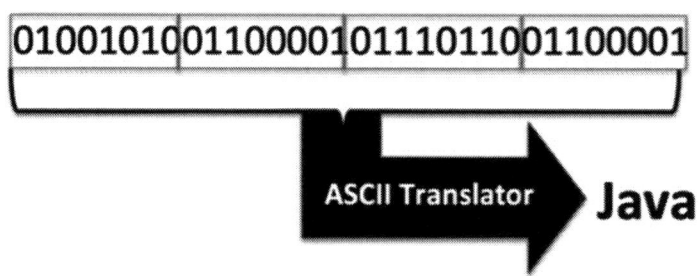

Following the same format to read base 10 numbers, each position in binary, or base 2, has the following values:

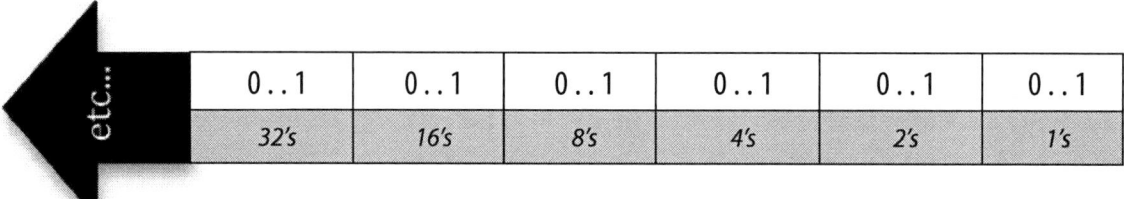

The pattern is straightforward: The rightmost position is always 1's. The next position to the left is 2 (for base 2) times that, or 2. The third position is 2 * 2 = 4, the fourth position is 4 * 2 = 8, etc.

A binary number can be converted to its decimal equivalent by reading from right to left and summing the values. The binary number 1010 converted to decimal:

$$(0 * 1) + (1 * 2) + (0 * 4) + (1 * 8) = 2 + 8 = 10$$

If you are given a decimal (base 10) number, you can convert it to binary (base 2) using the following approach. To convert the base 10 number 78 to binary, do the following. In each step, determine how many times two goes completely into the value (no fractions) and save the remainder:

1. Divide 78 by 2 (the base you are converting to)
   a. 78 / 2 = 39
   b. Save the remainder: 0

2. Divide the result of the previous step by 2
   a. 39 / 2 = 19
   b. Save the remainder: 1

3. Divide the result of the previous step by 2
   a. 19 / 2 = 9
   b. Save the remainder: 1

4. Divide the result of the previous step by 2
   a. 9 / 2 = 4
   b. Save the remainder: 1

5. Divide the result of the previous step by 2
   a. 4 / 2 = 2
   b. Save the remainder: 0

6. Divide the result of the previous step by 2
   a. 2 / 2 = 1
   b. Save the remainder: 0

7. Divide the result of the previous step by 2
   a. 1 / 2 = 0
   b. Save the remainder: 1
   c. STOP, because the result step 7a is 0

Now, pull the remainders in reverse order: 1001110

BASE 16

Base 16, or hexadecimal, is another importing number system in Computer Science. Because memory space is limited on computers, we want to store (or send) as much information we can in as small a memory space as possible. Hexadecimal numbers store large numbers with fewer digits than a base 10 or base 2 equivalent would require. Each position in a base 16 number has one of 16 possible values. Since we only have 10 possible digits (0 – 9) to work with, we also use the letters A – F:

0..9,A-F	0..9,A-F	0..9,A-F	0..9,A-F	0..9,A-F	0..9,A-F
1,048,576's	65,546's	4096's	256's	16's	1's

Just as with the other number systems, the rightmost position is always 1's. The second position is position 1's value times the base we are representing (16), or 16*1=16. The third position is 16*16=256, and so on.

A hexadecimal number can be converted to decimal by reading from right to left and summing the values. The hex number 2BA converted to decimal:

```
(A * 1) + (B * 16) + (2 * 256) = (10 * 1) + (11 * 16) + (2 * 256) = 698
```

To convert a decimal number to a hexadecimal number, use the same process (using remainders) that is used to convert from decimal to binary. To convert the base 10 number 843 to hexadecimal, do the following:

1. Divide 843 by 16 (the base you are converting to)
   a. 843 / 16 = 53
   b. Save the remainder: 11 (or B in Hex)

2. Divide the result of the previous step by 16

    a. 53 / 16 = 3

    b. Save the remainder: 5

3. Divide the result of the previous step by 16

    a. 3 / 16 = 0

    b. Save the remainder: 3

    c. STOP, because the result in step 3a is 0

Now, pull the remainders in reverse order: 35B